You are there at Madison Square Garden
with 20,000 people and
a white-clad choir of 2,000 singing

Billy Graham speaks to you

- about coming to know God
- about being radical
- about rebellion in youth
- about spiritual insight
- about returning to the faith
- about facing problems
- about religious truth in the scientific age

He says:

> "Receive Christ in your life. He will
> forgive your sins, and give you
> purpose and meaning in your life."

These are the ten sermons that stirred the largest nightly TV audience ever to follow a religious event, lightly edited for you to read and reread as inspiration.

**THE
CHALLENGE**
was originally published by Doubleday & Company, Inc.

Other books by Billy Graham

My Answer

Peace With God

The Secret of Happiness

World Aflame

Published by Pocket Books

 Are there paperbound books you want but cannot find in your retail stores?

You can get any title in print in:
Pocket Book editions • Pocket *Cardinal* editions • Permabook editions or Washington Square Press editions. Simply send retail price, local sales tax, if any, plus 15¢ to cover mailing and handling costs for each book wanted to:
MAIL SERVICE DEPARTMENT
   POCKET BOOKS • A Division of Simon & Schuster, Inc.
   1 West 39th Street   •   New York, New York 10018
   Please send check or money order. We cannot be responsible for cash.
   Catalogue sent free on request.

Titles in these series are also available at discounts in quantity lots for industrial or sales-promotional use. For details write our Special Projects Agency: The Benjamin Company, Inc., 485 Madison Avenue, New York, N.Y. 10022.

BILLY GRAHAM

The Challenge

*Sermons from
Madison Square Garden*

PUBLISHED BY POCKET BOOKS NEW YORK

THE CHALLENGE

Doubleday edition published November, 1969

Pocket Book edition published February, 1971

This *Pocket Book* edition includes every word
contained in the original, higher-priced edition. It is printed
from brand-new plates made from completely reset, clear, easy-to-read
type. *Pocket Book* editions are published by Pocket Books, a division
of Simon & Schuster, Inc., 630 Fifth Avenue, New York, N.Y. 10020.
Trademarks registered in the United States and other countries.

Standard Book Number: 671-75649-4.
Library of Congress Catalog Card Number: 78-100047.
Copyright, ©, 1969, by Billy Graham. All rights reserved.
This *Pocket Book* edition is published by arrangement with Doubleday &
Company, Inc.

Printed in the U.S.A.

CONTENTS

Introduction		vii
I.	Come and Know God	1
II.	The Other Death	13
III.	Man in Rebellion	27
IV.	The Prodigal Son	40
V.	Heaven and Hell	52
VI.	Truth and Freedom	66
VII.	Let's Be Radical	79
VIII.	Two Sets of Eyes	91
IX.	The Giants You Face	106
X.	The Day to Come	118

INTRODUCTION

The sermons contained in *The Challenge* were preached to audiences in Madison Square Garden, the Manhattan Center, and the Felt Forum in New York City. In addition, these services were telecast either live or rebroadcast the next evening in twenty-one cities from Boston to Miami along the eastern seaboard. In addition, three of these sermons were preached at prime evening time on more than three hundred TV stations throughout the United States and on an additional sixty stations abroad. It was the most unique and demanding communications venture we have ever undertaken. Because of the varied audiences, the talks had to be simple, clear, and to the point. This book contains, with only minor editing, the ten sermons just as they were given. No attempt has been made to make them what they are not—literary masterpieces. The spoken word is of necessity different from the written word. Someone once asked George Whitefield if he could print one of Whitefield's sermons. Whitefield said, "You may print it if you put in the thunder, the fire, and the lightning." It is impossible to capture in print the rapport, the camaraderies, and the banter of oral delivery between speaker and audience. In reading these sermons try to imagine yourself in the new Madison Square Garden with 20,000 people around you. Try to imagine some of the color, the various ethnic groups, the white-clad choir of two thousand, the TV cameras, and the flower-decked podium. Try, as I did, to visualize people listening in bars, in coffeehouses, in cafes, and in thousands of homes. Then listen not to Billy Graham, but to the challenge of God to modern man. Many people have written and said that after the first few minutes they were no longer conscious of the preacher, but they were listening to "another voice."

I pray that as you read these addresses that you may share some of the inspiration I experienced in giving them. May God bless you.

Billy Graham

The Challenge

*Sermons from
Madison Square Garden*

I.

COME AND KNOW GOD

Now, tonight I want you to turn with me to the 17th chapter of the Book of Acts. If you have your Bibles—and I hope you will bring your Bibles every night—our lesson is from the Book of Acts, the 17th chapter, the passage Dr. Kirkland read to us a few moments ago.

In this particular passage we find the Apostle Paul had gone to Athens. He is waiting for his friends to join him, and just as New York City is the communications, the intellectual and the cultural center—and certainly the financial center—of the United States, so Athens was the cultural and intellectual center of the ancient world. It was the city of Aristotle, Plato, Socrates and Epicurus. Paul had been very busy. He was very tired and needed a rest. But he took a walk through the streets of Athens.

Now the other night, with one of the cameramen from NBC, I took a walk through Times Square. The Bible says that when Paul took a walk through Athens, what he saw stirred him. Paul became very upset, and the Greek word used means that he was provoked. He was irritated. He was challenged. He was angry at what he saw. The Apostle Paul saw the moral corruption and the hundreds of idols in Athens. If we look about New York City today —and the other great cities of America—we see the materialism, the money, the obsession with sex, the pleasure, the leisure, the fashions, the entertainments, the ambition—all that we have made "gods" in our generation.

Eric Sevareid said the other night on television, "It is not doing us so much good to unravel the nature of the universe unless we can unravel the nature of man."

And that's what the Apostle Paul became convinced of

1

when he saw all that was happening in Athens. And I tell you that when I walk the streets of New York City, and when I walk the streets of the other great metropolitan areas of the western world, I, too, become stirred. I become challenged, and at times I become angry, and I become irritated at what I see. I see the vast social problems that we have not solved. Right here in Manhattan are some of the worst slums of the world side by side with some of the most luxurious places in all the world. I see the moral problems of our generation. I can walk down Times Square and see some of the filthiest pornography, both in motion pictures and in newsstands, that you can find anywhere in the world. And no nation in history has ever gone in for that type of immorality and escaped the judgment of God. We are in for the judgment of God unless we clean it up. God will not wink at our sins.

The people of Athens had lost faith in their gods, and Americans, too, are losing faith in their "gods." We have made materialistic gods. We made a god of science until science created the hydrogen bomb. We've made a goddess of sex, but with all our permissiveness, it hasn't brought happiness, peace or joy to our hearts. We have spiritual problems, the problem of boredom, the problem of loneliness. I read about a psychologist the other day who said that New York was the loneliest city in the world, and Dr. Stephen Olford, a pastor in this city, said that he believes loneliness is the greatest problem in New York City. How many lonely people are there searching for a friend in the midst of a great city?

You know, Jesus only wept three times. The Bible says that three times He shed tears. And one of those times He shed tears over Jerusalem. He said, "Jerusalem, Jerusalem. I could have gathered you under my wing as a hen would gather her chicks. I could have saved you. I could have solved your problem, but you would not let me. Therefore, Jerusalem, thou shalt be judged."

And I tell you this Crusade, I believe, has come at a crucial time in the history of this city and in the history of this nation, and unless our city and our nation repent, we will not be spared the judgment of God. City after city in the Bible was destroyed by the fires of judgment—Sodom, Babylon, Tyre, Sidon, Nineveh—because of their sins. And the same sins of those cities are the sins of the American city tonight and of the American people.

The Apostle Paul was so stirred that in spite of the fact that he needed a vacation, he began to talk to the people. He stood on the street corner in the "Times Square" of Athens and began to preach. He said, "Repent of your sins. Turn to God." He began to talk about Jesus Christ. He said, "Jesus Christ the Son of God has come. He died on the Cross for our sins, and God has raised Him from the dead. He can bring light to the city, light to your heart, change your life, give you a new motivation, give you a reason for existence."

Some of the intellectuals looked at him with disdain. They smiled and they sneered and some of them laughed and they said, "He's a babbler. He's a nitpicker. He doesn't know what he's talking about." Some of the people at the university became curious. They wanted to hear him. They wanted to hear what he had to say. They were always searching for something new, so they invited the Apostle Paul up to the Areopagus on Mars Hill to listen to an address and then to have dialogue with him and to ask him some questions. In the audience were some interesting people—the Epicureans were there. Epicurus was a great philosopher who had lived three hundred years earlier, and he had taught permissiveness, very much like we have it today. We call it the "new morality" today. There is nothing new about it at all. It is the old immorality disguised as the new morality. If you'll read the first chapter of Romans, you'll find a description of the so-called new morality. Ancient man deified his passions. Bacchus was the deification of his appetite. Venus and Aphrodite were the embodiment of sex. Mars and Jupiter represented the fighting, the warring, instinct. They were the gods of war.

Today man has outgrown the images of Bacchus, but he is still controlled by appetite. The Temple of Venus has been destroyed, but we are still dominated by passion. We've dismissed Mars as a creation of superstition, but the war gods are still with us, and man is still fighting. So all the old gods are still here. Man is still the same. The man that existed five thousand years ago has not changed. In Madison Square Garden he's the same. He has different style clothes, he speaks a different language, he has a sophistication about him and a façade about him, but his heart is the same. And I don't care if you go to Africa, or to China, or to Latin America, or to Europe, or to the Islands of the Sea, man is just the same. I don't find any difference between black, white, yellow, red; down underneath man is the same, the same loneliness, the same inward emptiness, the same search, the same quest, looking for peace and joy; looking for the meaning in human existence. And ancient man was the same, and that is why the Bible is so relevant tonight. That's why the Bible tonight speaks to modern man more than any book in the world, because it was written to men of all generations, because man never changes. Man's heart has always been the same.

The Bible says man is rebellious against God. The Bible says man is alienated from God. The Bible says man is cut off from God because of sin.

Now we had a report come out the other day about violence in the United States, and these reporters had spent a great deal of time, and had done a marvelous job explaining it. Somebody asked me on a television program, "Where do you think this violence comes from—this new form of violence that we have in America? Let me tell you, there is nothing new about it. Go back to the Garden of Eden. Cain murdered his brother Abel. That was the first act of violence, and all the way through the Bible, you will find violence. Through history you will find men killing, mugging, raping, hating—violent men. Why? Because man without God is "a violent man." He may be educated, but he becomes an educated savage. A Sing Sing warden once said he had enough Ph.D.s behind bars to staff a modern college. Why? Because we are separated from God, and without God we are restless, we cannot control our passions, and that's the reason if America forgets God we are going to become even far more violent. It is interesting to me that when we took God out of the public schools, we seemed to put violence and sex in, and the whole educational process began to flounder. And it seemed to come at the same time. As long as we honored God, as long as we told our young people that God mattered, that prayer was important, that morality meant something—it seemed to have a wholesome effect. But then we told them that morality doesn't count, morals are relative, and we told them the Bible isn't important any more. We told them they couldn't even pray, so they said, "To heck with the whole thing." Now they are rebelling, and we wonder what happened.

The Bible says, "You sow to the wind and you reap a whirlwind."

You know Carl Jung, the great psychologist, warned us that the evils of primitive men are still crouching in all of us, alive and ugly in the dark recesses of the heart under the sins of this era of civilization. And he said this: "Only Christianity is keeping them in check and if Christianity is neglected, the old horrors will come upon us again."

Yes, the Epicureans were there. They said, "Have a good time. Eat, drink and be merry."

The Stoics also were there. Now they were the intellectual leaders of that generation. I read an article the other day by a professor of Cornell University. He said, "Two years ago we sat in our ivory towers thinking we were the most intellectual group of men in all the world. We were arrogant and proud." He said, "All of our theories have come crashing down, and you've never met a more humble, humiliated faculty anywhere in America than the faculty of Cornell University."

Yes, the Stoics, the intellectuals, were there to listen to the Apostle Paul, for you see, Paul was an intellectual. But Paul had been humbled by Christ on the Road to Damascus. A bright light had shone, and the Apostle Paul had fallen down and in humility, like a little child, he said, "Who art thou, Lord?" And the Lord revealed Himself to him and the Apostle Paul, intellectual giant that he was, became as humble as a little child. Jesus said before you can ever come to Him, you have to repent of your sins. You have to be converted and become as a little child. That is what He was talking about. You may be a professor at the university, but before you can come to Christ, you have to become as a little child. You've got to have the faith of a little child in his father.

The Bible also says the gossipers were there. Now who were the gossipers? They were the people who talked a lot, but they said very little, and they listened very little.

You know we have on campus today a great deal of emotional intellectualism and emotional talk. When I was here twelve years ago they accused us of emotionalism. If you spoke a little bit loud, or if a person shed a tear, that was called emotionalism. I haven't been asked that question once since I've been here this time, because you see, the great university campuses are now right on the television screens and we see all the emotionalists at the intellectual centers. They are intellectual emotionalists.

Now there is nothing wrong with enthusiasm, and there is nothing wrong with emotion if it is in the right direction and under control. Jesus had emotion. We are to have feeling in our faith.

Then there was a group there listening to Paul that day who were the serious searchers after the truth. They really were wanting to know where they came from, why they were there, and where they were going. They wanted to know God. And you know that crowd today doesn't get very much time on the television screen. You know we've got six and a half million American students at universities and colleges. A hundred and thirty-five thousand are hard-core radicals, we are told. Another half million are in sympathy with them, but where are the six million that you don't hear about? There are millions of young people in America who are serious about an education. They are serious about life, and tens of thousands of them know Christ as their Lord and Savior.

We have here in this Crusade scores of students who have come from many universities across America to help. I wish you could see them. I wish you could hear them talk about Christ.

I was told last night by a lady who said, "You know I was coming down the elevator at the hotel and a fellow with a beard and long hair smiled at me and said, 'Lady, are you going to the Madison Square Garden Crusade?'" She said, "I nearly fell over, and he was so kind and so gracious, at first I couldn't get over it." But she said, "You know he looked like Jesus."

He's one of the fellows at this Crusade. He will be at the Manhattan Center after the service tonight helping over there in our youth meetings after the Garden services because we have a lot of fellows that are coming here from all over who believe in God and have a beard, also. My grandfathers, both of them, had beards. It's not whether you have a beard or not. It is whether you have Christ in your heart that counts.

Now Paul came to his sermon, and when he was on the way up to Mars Hill, he saw a plaque. It said, "To the Unknown God." Now they had hundreds and thousands of idols in Athens, but there was one they didn't know.

And do you know there are many people right here tonight who are the same way? You see, you know of the existence of God. Only a fool has said in his heart, "There is no God."

Eisenhower said, "It takes no brains to be an atheist. Any stupid person can deny the supernatural." I think General Eisenhower was correct.

We believe in God, but we don't know God. Do you know God? Could you actually look me in the eye and say tonight, "I know God. God lives in my heart. I talk to God. I love God. God answers my prayers. I know Him as my Lord and my Master and my Savior." Can you say that? You know about God. You may have an intellectual concept of God, but you don't really know God. So we have the "unknown God" in America—the God whom we believe in but don't know.

Well, I want to tell you that I had an experience with God a few years ago, and I've had a thousand experiences with Him since then. I know He is, and I know He lives in my heart. He's answered the great questions of my life.

He has brought a peace and a joy and a happiness to my heart. He can do the same for you, if you will let Him.

Then the Apostle Paul preached that great sermon on Mars Hill. He talked about the one true God who was the Creator of the world. Yes, there is one God, the Creator of the world.

Martin Luther King said, on April 13, 1960, these words:

"I have become more and more convinced of the reality of a personal God."

Is God personal to you—the mighty God of Creation? When those astronauts were out on the other side of the moon and they were showing pictures of our earth, and we realized there are hundreds and billions of planets and stars out there in space, one of my friends, who is a scientist at one of our universities, wrote me a letter and said, "I don't know how anyone could deny the existence of a supreme Intelligence when all of that is moving in absolute perfect precision and we only know a little bit. We are only touching the fringes of outer space."

Then the Apostle Paul said, "God has made of one blood all the nations of the world."

Now the Athenians were proud. They thought there was no one superior to them. They thought they were the superrace.

I want to tell you the Bible says there is no superior race. We are one blood. We may have dark skin, we may have yellow skin—God made us that way. God made some people black and some people white and some people brown and some people yellow. God made us that way. Let's accept it and be proud of it. Black is beautiful. White is beautiful. Yellow is beautiful, if Christ is in our heart. We are one blood, we are one human race with a soul responsible before God. Unless we solve our problems and solve them pretty quick there won't be any white, yellow, red and black to argue and fight about. We will all be gone.

We are one blood. I know there are racial tensions around the world. The Chinese and Malays out in Singapore have been fighting it out, and the problem is race. It's not an American problem; it's a world problem. But, "God has made of one blood all nations," the Scripture says, "under heaven." And the Bible says as Christians we have the power to love each other. But I don't believe that we are ever going to get the power to love each other across this nation until we all come to know Christ. Christ can give us the supernatural power to love a person of another race. Christ can do it.

And then Paul said, "God is not far away." Now there were some people in Athens who thought God dwelt way off somewhere on Mount Olympus. But Paul said, "No, God is here. God is not on a mountain. God is not on a star. God is not on another planet. God is right here on this earth, and God is not very far away from any of you. He can be with you in your loneliness. He can help you in your sickness. He can take your guilt away. He can help you in your frustrations. He can give answers to the mysteries and the problems and the difficulties of life."

Then Paul reaches the very heart of his sermon. He says this, and this is what I want every person in this audience tonight to hear. Listen to this if you've never listened in your life. This is the Word of God:

The great Apostle Paul was saying, "God now commands all men everywhere"—think of it now, we are all one blood—"He commands all Africans, all Europeans, all Asians, all New Yorkers, all Northerners, all Southerners, all Westerners, all Easterners—God commands all men everywhere to repent."

God doesn't say, "I suggest you repent." God doesn't say, "I advise you to repent." God doesn't say, "I hope you repent." God says, "I *command* you to repent."

And I want to ask the question tonight, have you repented? God demands it! That is a command of God. Nothing else counts in this life or in the life to come unless you have obeyed that one great command, *repent*!

You know there is a top tune now on all of the juke boxes, "Turn, Turn, Turn." That's repentance. Turn. Turn around. Change. Change your mind. Change your way of living. Change your idea about God. Change your idea about yourself. Change your idea about your neighbor. Turn around. That's repentance.

Has there been a change in your life? The Bible says, "Old things shall pass away. Everything in your life shall become new. You should become a brand new creation in Christ."

Has that happened to you? You go to church. Perhaps you believe in the Golden Rule. Perhaps you even accept the Ten Commandments as your moral guide, but that's not enough. You must repent, and everybody in this audience has something he can repent of. Think a little bit. Is there one single person in this audience who doesn't need to repent? No.

The Bible says, "All have sinned and come short of the glory of God."

Is there one single person sinless in the world? No.

"All have sinned and come short of the glory of God."

Then if you have sinned, you have something to repent of, because repentance means that you confess to God that you have sinned. It means that you say, "Oh, God, I have sinned. I am willing to change my way of living. I am ready to turn from my sin."

Now why does God command you to repent? That's the next sentence. Why does God command you to repent? Listen:

"Because he has appointed a day."

Notice, God has appointed a day, an exact day, in which He will judge the world in righteousness "by that man whom he hast ordained."

Now you and I in 1969 don't like to think of God in terms of wrath and anger and judgment and hell. You see, we try to remake God to conform to our own image. We try to make God as we think He ought to be. That's idolatry.

There is an article in a current magazine this month by a man who left the Catholic Church. In that article he denies the revelation about God in the Bible. He formed a God in his own mind. No wonder he left the church. He no longer believed in the God of Christianity.

When we were here twelve years ago Bishop James

Pike was then Dean of St. John's Cathedral here in New York and Bishop Pike left the church recently. He wrote an article as to why he left, and it seems to me that there were three reasons why he left: because of his inability to find credibility, relevance and performance. To him Christianity was no longer credible, or Christ was not, or the church was not . . . no longer relevant, and the performance was not there.

Well, I want to tell you I found exactly the opposite. Jesus Christ is credible! In Jesus Christ I find the whole Gospel and the Bible the most relevant book in the world. In Christ I find Him performing everything He ever promised to do, and He can do it in your life if you put your trust in Him.

Now God has commanded us to repent because He is going to judge the world. Yes, a judgment day is coming. Jesus said, "Every idle word that men shall speak, they shall give an account in the day of judgment." Think of it! Every idle word that you speak, every thought, every intent, everything that you ever did in the dark, everything that you swept under the rug, everything that you thought had been hidden, will all be brought to light at the judgment, and we are going to be judged by that man —that man, the Lord Jesus Christ. He came the first time as the gentle Savior. Next time He comes as the judge of all the earth, and the Bible says the proof of the fact that God is going to judge the world is that God raised Him from the dead.

Now you may laugh. They laughed at Noah. They laughed at Jeremiah. They laughed at Lot. They laughed at Amos. They laughed at the Apostles. They've laughed at the preachers down through the centuries when they warned of coming judgment, but that didn't keep the judgment back.

Judgment is coming. You are going to face it. Are you ready?

Amos the prophet said, "Prepare to meet thy God."

God has raised Him from the dead, and the Christ I present tonight is not the Christ on the Cross. He died on the Cross for our sins. He shed His blood for our sins, and every time we take communion in our churches we remember the blood that was shed. Without the shedding of that blood there is no forgiveness of our sins. But that is not the total Gospel. The Gospel is that Christ has been raised from the dead, and I now have Good News! Death has been conquered. Christ is alive. He is coming back again, and He is going to set up His kingdom. That's the message Paul preached that day.

What happened? The same thing that will happen here exactly. There were three reactions. First, some laughed and scoffed. The second group said, "Well, we'll hear again of this matter. We'd like to think it over." They put it off. Now that's very dangerous, because, you see, you may never hear the Gospel preached again quite like this. And it's dangerous because if you do hear it, the soil of your heart may be different. You see, you can only come to God when the Holy Spirit draws you. Now thousands of people around the world have been praying for this meeting tonight. Your heart in a strange way has been moved, and challenged and convicted, and disturbed tonight, and the Bible says, "Now is the acceptable time; today is the day of salvation." The Bible warns that you can harden your heart so you should come and make your commitment to Christ now while the Spirit of God is speaking. You may never be this close to the kingdom of God again.

So, there were some that laughed. Some of you will walk out of here laughing and sneering and saying, "What a fool!" Some of you will say, "Well, I'd like to think this over a few days." Others will make a commitment tonight, and that's what happened when Paul preached his great sermon.

You know there is a slogan in the *Daily Telegraph* of London. I get the *Telegraph* in my home. It says, "You can't change the facts, but you can change your mind."

You know when Apollo 11 will be taken to the launching pad, it is going to go one mile per hour to the launching pad. Then when it blasts off it will go up to 24,000 miles per hour. But that first mile will take an hour—to get it to the launching pad.

Tonight you start to the launching pad, and you may have to move slowly and falteringly and your faith may be small, but your faith is centered in the Person of the Lord Jesus Christ.

This past week thousands of American university students went forward to receive their diplomas publicly. I am asking you tonight to come forward publicly to receive Christ. Let Him forgive your sins. Let Him come into your hearts and give you a new life and a new dimension of living and leave here tonight knowing that your name is written in the Book of Life. Leave here knowing that you will never have to face the judgment, knowing that all of your sins are forgiven, knowing that you are going to heaven when you die, with a new power to face the problems and the difficulties that you face in your life. How are we going to do it?

I am going to ask hundreds of you to get out of your seats all over this great stadium from wherever you are and come and stand in front of this platform. . . .

Delivered June 13, 1969

II.

THE OTHER DEATH

I'm going to ask that we bow our heads in prayer. Every head bowed and every eye closed in prayer. On this Sunday evening there are hundreds of people in this auditorium who need to make the commitment to Christ that Jerome Hines made fifteen years ago. You, too, have a sense of guilt and frustration and confusion in your life. The problems are just too great for you to cope with. Real hangups. You need help. There's an uncertainty about death. You're not sure where you're going if you died. You can find an answer tonight right here by making your commitment to Jesus Christ who died on the Cross for you.

Our Father and our God, we pray that thy Holy Spirit will speak to our hearts tonight and convince us of sin and righteousness and judgment and point us to the Lamb of God that taketh away the sin of the world. For we ask it in His name. Amen.

Tomorrow night will be young people's night again, and I will speak to all the teenagers and their parents. I think their parents need it sometimes more than they do, so I hope that you will come tomorrow night.

I wish I had a voice like Bev Shea and a speaking voice and a singing voice like Jerome Hines. I don't know whether many of you know I actually started out my ministry as a song leader, and I took voice lessons. I don't know whether you knew that, Bev. I've been with Bev Shea now twenty-five years and there are certain secrets I've kept from him. And I took voice lessons until the fifth lesson when a hound dog outside began to bark and the voice teacher told me that he thought I must have other gifts.

So I started preaching and I prepared four sermons and I thought that each sermon would last about an hour. And I preached my first sermon in a small church in northern Florida. About thirty people were present. And I was so frightened and so scared that I preached all four sermons in eight minutes.

Now because of television my sermons have to be short. I think all of you have heard about the man who was introduced and he was supposed to speak for twenty minutes and he spoke for an hour, and after an hour and twenty minutes he was still speaking. The man who introduced him could stand it no longer and he picked up the gavel and threw it at the speaker. And it missed the speaker and hit the man on the front row. And as the man was going into unconsciousness he said, "Hit me again. I can still hear him."

But tonight I want you to turn with me to Hebrews, the

ninth chapter and the 22nd verse. Hebrews 9:22. These words: "And almost all things are by the law purged with blood; and without the shedding of blood there is no forgiveness."

What a strange verse! ". . . without the shedding of blood there is no forgiveness." Without the shedding of blood, sin cannot be forgiven. Well you say, "I thought that went out with the barbarians."

You know it's a very interesting thing to me. I took my work in college in anthropology and I wrote a thesis one day on the subject of blood in the various religions of the world, and you know, it's very difficult to find any part of the world where blood sacrifices have not been made. As a matter of fact, among the Aztecs of ancient Mexico more than 20,000 human beings were slaughtered every year on their altars to their gods, to appease their gods, to purge themselves of guilt. And all over the world, wherever you go, not only was there animal sacrifice but human sacrifice to appease the gods. Where did this concept come from? And certainly if you're Jewish and if you go through the Old Testament and read the Talmud, it's filled with blood. Thousands upon thousands of goats and lambs and bullocks were killed and slaughtered on Jewish altars every year.

Then you come to Christianity. Two hundred and fifty-five times in the New Testament it talks about blood. Now isn't that something sort of strange? And if you're a member of other religions of the world, blood plays a prominent place. Why is that?

We were reading a few weeks ago about thirty million young Red Chinese guards marching down the streets of Peking and they were screaming and chanting—and wasn't it interesting what they were chanting? They were chanting this verse: "Without the shedding of blood there will be no revolution." That was their slogan. That's what they were chanting—thirty million Red Guards chanting "Without the shedding of blood there is no revolution."

I was in Moscow some time ago and I asked the guide of Intourist who was showing us around, "What does the Red Star mean with its five points?" And she had an interesting answer. She said, "The five points point to the five continents of the world. The red stands for blood that will have to be shed to bring about revolution on all five continents."

We're getting used to blood because we see it on our television screens and we certainly see it in the motion picture houses. Vietnam is a shedding of blood. The highways of America are a shedding of blood every day. Crime is a shedding of blood. Right here on Manhattan Island more people are murdered in cold blood every year than in all of Great Britain combined with its fifty million population.

One of the most popular best-seller books made into a motion picture was entitled *In Cold Blood,* and yet, Judaism and Christianity have been called bloody religions. Some years ago I preached all over Israel and my subject in preaching was "Why I'm a Christian." I said I think that if an Islamic leader or Hindu leader comes to the United States we would like to hear why he's a Hindu or why he's a Moslem. I said, "I'm a Christian. Wouldn't you like to know why I'm a Christian?" And I went back into the Old Testament and brought it right through all the blood that had been shed on the altars in Judaism. You see in Leviticus, the 17th chapter, one of the most important passages in all of literature says this: "For the life of the flesh is in the blood and I've given it to you upon the altar to make an atonement for your souls, for it is the blood that makes an atonement for the soul."

Now this blood stands for life. It represents life. Life has to be given as an atonement for sin.

Science doesn't know what life is yet. Science is not even sure exactly when death takes place, but we know that it has something to do with the blood. Every one of us has about five quarts of blood and it circulates every twenty-three seconds so that every cell in our body is constantly supplied and cleansed at the same time. This same blood, every twenty-three seconds, carries all the garbage out without any contamination. Think of it now, the same bloodstream that carries the food to the cell carries the garbage out, all within twenty-three seconds. Just the study of the blood alone should convince any normal person that there must be a divine intelligence.

The most mysterious substance of the body is the blood, and the Bible says it's the life of the flesh. Without blood you cannot live. You have to have blood. I wish we had time to go into it a little bit further tonight as to what blood really is to your body. But the Bible says all of us are related by blood to Adam and the Scripture says God has made of one blood all nations that dwell on the face of the earth. All of us here tonight, whether you're black, white, yellow, red, rich, poor, whatever language you speak, we're all related to Adam by blood. It is Adam's blood that courses in every man's veins, whoever he is, whatever he is. And this blood that you have in your body carries with it a sentence of death.

The Bible says, "Wherefore as by one man's sin entered into the world and death by sin and so death passed on all men for all have sinned." Adam rebelled against God. His bloodstream became poisoned and every one of us as sons and daughters of Adam have blood poisoning and that's the problem with the world tonight—blood poisoning. Our blood has been poisoned by a disease called sin, and it ultimately ends in death.

You're going to die. The Bible says, "It's appointed unto man once to die." Go out to the graveyard. It testifies that the Bible is right. Man does die. I don't care what a man's name is. His name may be Roosevelt, it may be Churchill, it may be Clark Gable, it may be Marilyn Monroe, it may be Adlai Stevenson, it may be Senator Kennedy. Death comes. All of us are going to die. The life of the flesh is in the blood, but something's wrong with the blood. Something's wrong with the heart. It has a disease that causes death eventually.

But there's another death because there's a spiritual application. The blood is only a symbol of life. When it is shed, death occurs. It also brings about a spiritual death that is very real. A separation from God that Jesus called "hell." Because to every one of us it is appointed unto man once to die and after that the judgment. God is going to judge us because of sin. Death and hell are going to be cast into the lake of fire, the Bible says. With all that this means, whether it's symbolic or literal, it's terrible and it's a penalty because of the sin that is in our bloodstream.

Arnold Toynbee has written a book entitled *Man's Concern with Death,* and he says death is man's greatest enemy. And in a recent Gallup Poll we've been reading about a departure from religious faith in the United States. But in another recent Gallup Poll, did you know that five percent more Americans believe in life after death now than they did twenty years ago?

Pope Paul said some time ago that the world is in the throes of an unprecedented and sinister force of evil and everyone is being dragged away and overcome by the irresistible current as though by a river, that carries us away.

The popular young novelist Susan Sontag from Oxford and the Sorbonne in Paris said, "The United States is a doomed country. I only pray that when America falls, it doesn't drag the rest of the planet down, too."

I read the other day about a tiger in India that went on a five-day rampage and ate five people. The Bible teaches that in the bloodstream of New York, in the bloodstream of America, in the bloodstream of all of humanity, there's a tiger—sin, is a lurking tiger waiting to devour and it's within each one of us. We all have this "tiger in our tank." We're sinners and the penalty of our rebellion and our sin is death.

When you come to the Old Testament you find it all the way through. Go back to Adam and Eve. Remember Adam and Eve were in a perfect Paradise. They were created in the image of God. God never meant that they would ever see death. God never meant we should die. He never meant that anybody should get sick. He never meant anybody ever to be murdered. He never meant that anybody would ever have to fight in a war. Everything was perfect. God gave man the freedom of choice, and God said, "If you obey me and love me and serve me, you'll live forever and we'll build a wonderful world. But if you disobey me and rebel against me, you're going to die." Man thought about it. One day man rebelled against

THE OTHER DEATH 19

God, he broke God's law, and God kept His word. Man has been dying ever since.

And so God wanted to do something about it and God set about to redeem and to save man. And so God came, the Bible says, to the Garden of Eden and said, "Adam, where are you?" And Adam was hiding. He was naked. He had gone and gotten some fig leaves and sewed them together and clothed himself, trying to hide his nakedness and his sin and his rebellion from God, but he couldn't do it. That's like a lot of people today. We're doing everything in the world to try to hide from God. We go on trips of alcohol and sex and dope. Actually we are trying to run away from reality. We're trying to run away from God. We're trying to hide somewhere, but "the Hound of Heaven" is there. Always disturbing, always bothering. We try to escape. We become slaves of sin and habit trying to get away from God.

But Adam and Eve could not hide from God. And the Bible says that God went out and slew some animals, took their skins, and clothed Adam and Eve. You see in the beginning God never meant we were to wear clothes. Now they're trying to undress people here on Times Square in the motion picture and on the stage. God never intended you to have clothes. Sin is what brought about the necessity for clothes. We have abused by sin God's great gift of sex, and God clothed our first parents after they sinned. They were originally in a state of innocence, and as long as they were innocent they were not conscious of the fact they were naked. God clothed them, but blood had to be shed for their disobedience, and from the very beginning God was saying, "Without the shedding of blood there is no forgiveness."

Cain and Abel were the first children of Adam and Eve. Cain brought a sacrifice to God. He was very religious, but his offering was not acceptable to God. Why? Because it was nothing but vegetables. Abel, his brother, came and brought a blood sacrifice and God accepted it. God was saying right in the beginning, "You have to come by blood."

"Noah built an altar unto the Lord and took of every

clean beast and every clean fowl and offered an offering on the altar."

Remember the story of Abraham taking Isaac to Mount Moriah, there where Jerusalem now stands? God had told Abraham to take his son and offer him as an offering. Abraham, in complete obedience to God and loyalty to what God said, was about to slay his own son, and as the knife was descending, the angel of the Lord caught his hand and stopped him. But that's how far Abraham was prepared to go with God.

Sometimes God will test us almost to that point to see if we really are serious about our commitment to Jesus Christ. Abraham was willing to give his son. And the son said, "Father, where is the sacrifice?" He didn't know he was the sacrifice. And a ram was caught in the bushes and the ram became the substitute. Blood was shed.

Or, remember that night in Egypt that Jews to this day still celebrate? The Passover. And remember that God said, "I'm going to destroy the first-born in all of Egypt and I want you to go out and slay a lamb and take the blood and put it on the doorpost and when I see the blood, I'll pass over." Not when I see your good resolutions, not when I see your tears, not when I see your agonies, not when I see your good works. When I see the "blood" sprinkled there by faith.

God took blood, which is something ugly, something that's repulsive, to show us how ugly, how repulsive, and how terrible our sins are in His sight, and it becomes a symbol of the cleansing from sin. "When I see the blood I will pass over."

There are many people who join a church and they think that's enough. Many people get baptized and think that's enough. Many people try to live by the Golden Rule and they say that's enough. Many people try to give money. That's fine. All of these things are good, but they are not enough. The blood has to be sprinkled there by faith. "When I see the blood I will pass over."

When I stand at the entrance to the kingdom of heaven and they ask me for the password, do you know what I'm going to answer? I'm not going to say, "Lord, I preached

THE OTHER DEATH

to great crowds of people." I'm not going to say, "Lord, I read the Bible through." I'm not going to say, "Lord, I was married to a wonderful Christian woman. I'm coming in on her good works." I'm going to say, 'Lord, I plead the blood, for the blood of Jesus Christ His Son cleanseth from all sin."

Why is it there's a Cross on every Catholic and Protestant church? Why is it that a priest wears a Cross? Why is it that when you go and take communion you drink wine? What does that wine symbolize? Blood! That's what you do when you take communion and that's the very heart of Christianity. The communion is the heart of our worship.

John the Baptist cried out. What did he say? "Behold the Lamb of God." Why did he say "Lamb"? Our Lord Jesus Christ was "The Lamb" predicted all the way through the Old Testament. The 53rd chapter of Isaiah tells us how He died eight hundred years before He was born. He wept over Jerusalem. He sweat drops of blood in the Garden of Gethsemane. And then He went to the Cross and they put spikes in His hands and a crown of thorns on His brow and a spear in His side, and blood came. And all the way through the New Testament we find the expression "the blood of Jesus," "the blood of Christ." Fourteen times Jesus mentioned His own blood. He predicted His own death. He told Nicodemus, "As Moses lifted up the serpent in the wilderness, even so must the son of man be lifted up." Blood is mentioned 255 times.

Why? Because when Jesus Christ died on that Cross, the possibility of our salvation was accomplished by His death, by the shedding of His blood, by His paying the penalty and paying the price. The penalty for our sin and rebellion is death. Jesus stepped out and said, "I'll take that death." He voluntarily laid down His life and took the penalty which we deserve. That's what the Cross is all about; that's what the communion table at the worship service of your church, Catholic or Protestant, is all about.

The blood of Christ also redeems us. 1 Peter 1:18: "For as much as ye know that ye were not redeemed with corruptible things, as silver and gold, from your vain conversation received by tradition from your fathers; but with the precious blood of Christ, as of a lamb without blemish and without spot." You weren't redeemed with gold. God didn't save you by silver. God didn't save you by good works. God saved you by the blood.

Now redemption means buying someone from slavery. Jesus said, "I've come to give my life a ransom for many." And when He said this nobody needed to explain it because half of the world in that day was in slavery. Now here's an interesting thing. The slaves of that day were not black as they were in America 150 years ago. The slaves were white. I can trace my ancestry right on back to northern Europe and my ancestors way, way, way back were slaves. Every group of people in the world has at some time or other been in slavery. The Jewish people were in slavery to the Egyptians for four hundred years. And Peter said Christ buys you back by His own blood. From what? From the slavery of sin.

You see Jesus said, "Whosoever committeth sin is the slave of sin." How many people in this audience tonight are actually a slave of some habit? You're a slave of sin.

I was talking to a fellow the other day. He already knows that he has cancer of the lung. He held up a little white cigarette and said, "This has been my master for thirty years." He said, "I've tried to break this habit for thirty years and cannot and this little thing right here . . ." and he began to swear and said, "This is my master."

Did you read Somerset Maugham's *Of Human Bondage?* And read how he rejected God and then became a slave to sin? A friend of mine right here in New York City has written a book. He tells in this book how he rejected God and now he's a slave to passion and lust. He's a slave. He needs to be bought back; he needs to be set free. And the Bible says Christ can set you free tonight.

If you don't know Christ, you're in slavery, you're in bondage to sin. Christ can set you free. "If the Son therefore shall make you free, ye shall be free indeed."

Did you read the other day about that eighteen-year-old boy in Tennessee? He was in jail and he tried to cut his way out. He got a hole nine inches wide cut and then he put some grease all over his body. He got halfway through, and got stuck and had to call for help. He was in there several hours.

You know, many of us are trying to escape. We're trying to get out through drugs, we're trying to get out through a sex experience, we're trying to get out through alcohol, we're trying to get out in a thousand different ways, but we can't. We are stuck. We're in human bondage. We're slaves.

Christ died on the Cross to set you free; shed His blood to set you free. Only Christ can bring deliverance in this world and the world to come.

Secondly, we are justified by the blood. You say, what in the world does that word "justified" mean? In Romans 5 it says, "Much more now being justified by His blood, we shall be saved from wrath." Justified means more than forgiveness. I can say "I forgive you," but I can't justify you. Suppose you do something against me. Suppose you mugged me or robbed me. I can forgive you, but I can't justify you. God places you in His sight as though you'd never committed a single sin. You're just as clean and just as pure as the purest virgin who ever lived. The Bible says, "Though your sins be as scarlet they shall be as white as snow." No matter what your sins are, no matter how bad you've been, God not only forgives the past, but he clothes you in righteousness, the garment of the Lord Jesus Christ, as though you'd never even committed a sin. It's a wonderful thing to go to bed and know that. I go to bed every night, and I say, "Thank you, Lord, I'm justified. I'm not only forgiven, I'm justified. I'm going to heaven because I'm clothed in the righteousness of Jesus Christ." I didn't deserve it. I didn't buy it. It's free! God gives it! But it cost God the blood of His Son on the Cross.

Thirdly, the blood of Christ makes us all equal. One tongue, one language, one race. You see, the blood in the body is life. Christ talks about a body. The moment you receive Jesus Christ as your Savior—I don't care who you are—you become a member of the body of Christ. Christ is the head of the body, and it means that we're all equal members of the same body.

It doesn't matter what your skin color is. It doesn't matter what your social background is, or your national background. When we're in the body of Christ, we're all one. The middle wall of partition has been broken down. That's the solution ultimately to the race problem. One in Jesus, cleansed by the blood. The Bible says, "He hath broken down the middle wall of partition—and hath made one." How wonderful it is to have brothers and sisters, members of the same body, all over the world. No matter what the color of their skin—sometimes I can't talk their language. I've walked some of the trails of Africa, I've walked some of the roads in India, I couldn't speak a word of their language. But, oh my, the light on their face and the pat on the shoulder and the hug around the waist. One in Christ! Oh, the love that Christ brings!

Fourthly, the blood of Christ brings *peace,* and he has made peace through the blood of His Cross. Man craves peace. We all want peace. And we cry, "Peace, peace, peace, peace!" And we've had fifty-one wars since the Second World War. You see, what man really needs is peace with God. Man is at war with God. We're against God's program and God's will for our lives. We don't want to live disciplined lives under the Lordship of Christ. We need reconciliation to God. We need to be brought back to Him.

Fifthly, the Bible says also, that the blood of Christ cleanses. "Unto Him that loved us and washed us from all our sins in His own blood." You know a lady told me the other day that Jesus never mentioned the blood. She must have never read Matthew 26:28, "For this is my blood of the New Testament which is shed for many for the forgiveness of sins." That's what Jesus said.

What about you? Have you been cleansed by the blood? Have you been justified? Are you sure of it? Have you been reconciled to God and have you been reconciled to your fellow man? Yes, someday we shall overcome. But how? Oh, it tells us in Revelation 12:11, "They overcame by the blood of the Lamb." Not our blood, His blood. We shall overcome, and we shall stand in His presence, and the angels in heaven are going to sing, and all of us are going to join in singing with them, and the orchestras are going to play, and the choirs of heaven will shout. We will have overcome by the blood of the Lamb.

I'm going to heaven and I believe I'm going by the blood. I know that's not popular preaching. You don't hear much about that any more, but I'll tell you it's all the way through the Bible and I may be the last fellow on earth who preaches it, but I'm going to preach it because it's the only way we're going to get there.

You know we have blood banks. Nobody seems to mind that. The Red Cross means blood. I had a blood transfusion about three years ago that helped save my life, and I was thankful for the blood bank at the hospital. Well, there's an eternal blood bank, a heavenly blood bank, that we can apply to by faith, and it will take our guilt and sin away.

You know heart transplants are the medical sensation of our time, but there are two factors necessary for their success or failure. First, there must be a donor. In this case Jesus was the donor. He gave His life, He gave His heart, for you.

And then secondly, the patient must accept or reject the heart he receives. There is always the danger that the body may reject the new heart. But God has given you the ability and the right to choose. You can accept or you can reject. Which will you do?

If there's a doubt in your heart tonight that you're ready to meet God, I hope you'll receive Christ as your Savior. You say, "Well, Billy, what do I have to do?" You have to be willing to repent of your sins. That means to give up your sins. You have to say to God, "I'm a sinner. I'm sorry." You have to be willing to receive Jesus Christ by faith. Notice I said by faith. Tonight I've only touched the edge of this subject that runs through the Bible, this crimson thread from Genesis to Revelation. You may not understand all about it, and you may not understand any theology at all. You don't have to understand anything except that you're a sinner, and Christ died for you, and you're ready to receive Him. That's all you have to understand. You have to understand that God loves you and God wants to forgive you. You may be a Catholic or a Protestant or a Jew. Or you may not have any religion. But you want to come and let Jesus Christ into your heart tonight, and commit your life to Him and know that your sins are forgiven, you want to know that you're justified, and know that you're reconciled to God, and know that your name is written in the Book of Life, and know that you're going to heaven.

I'm going to ask you to make that decision. I'm going to ask you to get up out of your seats, all over this vast arena, and come and stand in front of this platform and stand here quietly. And after you've all come I'm going to say a word to you and have a prayer with you. Then a counselor will say a word to you and you can go back and join your friends.

Why do I ask you to come forward publicly? We do everything else in public. But in addition to that Jesus said, "If you're not willing to acknowledge me before men, I'll not acknowledge you before my Father." There's something about coming forward publicly out from the crowd and saying, "I receive Christ." It settles it in your heart.

I'm going to ask you to come. If you're with friends or relatives, they'll wait. You may be a member of the church; you may not be a member of any church. If you come from the top balcony up there, you have to go back and then down and around. An usher will show you. But all the other people can come straight down to the front and just come and stand here. Young man, young woman, father, mother. Whoever you are, whatever you are, God has spoken to you tonight. You get up and come right now and I'm going to ask that all of us be in an attitude of prayer as people come right now. Quickly, and just stand here reverently and say "Tonight I want Christ."

Delivered June 14, 1969

III.

MAN IN REBELLION

I'm going to ask that we bow our heads in prayer. Every head bowed and every eye closed in prayer. I'm going to ask that everyone be in an attitude of reverence and prayer. There are hundreds of people here tonight who have come with burdens that need to be lifted, problems that need to be solved, and guilt that needs to be taken away. You're searching for fulfillment in life, for purpose and meaning in your life. Many of you have problems concerning hangups of various sorts—the problem of marriage, the problem of a career, the problem of an education, the problem of military duty. All of these are problems that young people face.

Well, I want to tell you tonight you can find a peace and a joy and a sense of fulfillment by surrendering your life to Christ. And I'm going to ask you to listen quietly and reverently and no moving around and no whispering.

Our Father and our God, we pray that Thy Holy Spirit will draw to Thyself those whose hearts Thou hast prepared for this hour, for we ask it in Christ's name. Amen.

Now tonight I want you to turn with me to 2 Timothy, the third chapter, the passage that Roger Hull, Jr., read a few moments ago. In this passage Jesus is talking about the last days. Now, you will find that expression all the way through the Bible, especially the New Testament, and especially the teachings of Jesus. He talked about the last days, and He gave us some characteristics that would take place in the last days. Now, what does that "last days" mean? It means that as we move toward the end of history as we know it, not the end of the world, not the end of the earth, but the end of a stage of history that we're now in, the age of the working of the Spirit of God, the age of grace—as we move toward the end of that, there are going to be certain characteristics; and one of those characteristics is going to be world-wide lawlessness, world-wide crime, world-wide rebellion, especially on the part of young people.

Now many people have been disturbed about what has been taking place during the past few weeks in the United States on the campuses. It's not limited to the United States. Governor Rockefeller's visit to Latin America indicated that it's all through Latin America. Czechoslovakian students were demonstrating all last summer to gain freedom from what they considered to be suppression. All over the world young people are marching and demonstrating and lashing out and rebelling. And many people are asking the question, "Why? What happened?"

John Kenneth Galbraith was quoted in *The New York Times* this morning as saying this: "I am struck by the gloom that pervades modern university communities. It's a widely held view," he said, "that Harvard's tottering on the brink. One slight further nudge and it will tumble into the Charles River."

A twenty-one-year-old girl at college wrote her complaints recently and they were published. I think that her complaints register the thoughts of the current generation. Listen to them. Remember she's twenty-one, in college, and here's what she said: "At nineteen we're ready to die. We spend our youth chafing in the bonds of the protectivism that smothers and suppresses us. We strike out like little children throwing a tantrum. Our weapons are many: rejection of our parents, the flaunting of our illicit sex lives. The rebellion that seethes in youth today," she says, "has no foundation. They rebel against they know not what. They are searching for something, but what the something is they cannot say. We see our fathers and mothers scheming and debasing themselves, ignoring the values they offer to us as sacred, if they bother to do it at all. What are we to do except reject this hypocrisy? We are the hope of the world, but we have no hope. We only have hope in ourselves, and who are we? We cannot even discover."

John Kennedy, before he died, in a speech said this: "It is the fate of this generation to live with a struggle we did not start in a world we did not make. The pressures of life are not always distributed by choice."

Revolt and restlessness are everywhere on campus today. The whole educational process is now in jeopardy. Three hundred fifty colleges and universities are looking for presidents this summer and a thousand colleges and universities are looking for deans this summer; and Senator McCarthy said, "It's harder to be president of a university than to be President of the United States." He went on to say that when he was a young fellow, the boys used to chase the girls. He said now the girls chase college presidents.

And I heard about one fellow who wrote his parents, and he said that next year he did not want his regular allowance. He wanted combat pay.

Now questions are being asked. What's wrong? Where did we fail? Who are the rebels? What do they want? Where is it leading? Now I hope that you'll always keep in mind that only a relatively small minority of the seven million university and college students in America are revolting. 135,000 are considered radicals. 500,000 are sympathizers, but there are millions that are uncommitted. They haven't chosen the flag they're going to follow yet. They haven't chosen the creed they're going to believe in yet. Many of them are unhappy, they're confused, and they're frustrated. Thousands of them are hung up on sex and dope and alcohol.

But you know, today's youth is the first generation to grow up with modern parents. This is the first postmodern generation; and when they reached the age of awareness, they found waiting for them the jet airplane, the nuclear bomb, the television set, the computer, the pill, the space capsule, and a vaccine that wiped out one of the great cripplers of young people. They found LSD and marijuana on the street corner. They watched an adult society in which drinking had become a status symbol in the suburbs and sex jokes the norm of mixed-company parties. Most of all, they entered a life where science was supposed to be transcendent. So this generation of young people have grown up with affluency, technology, rapid social change, and violence. And they've been bombarded by television from childhood with suggestions of false needs, and this has created an expectation gap. They want these things they see on television, and they want them now.

And they've grown up with a system of education, part of which came from right here in New York City at the turn of the century, an experiment in education. This new type of education said that truth is something that the individual must discover for himself. Truth is not objective, but subjective. Everything is relative. "Is it true for me? Is it true for you?" they ask. They reject the statement of Jesus, Who said, "I am the Way, the Truth, and the Life." They reject His words, "Ye shall know the truth, and the truth shall make you free," because there is no such thing as absolute truth—so they said.

And so the philosophy of much of modern education was to guide students into an experience out of which they could deduce certain true propositions for themselves. So this led us into what has now become the permissive society. And all you have to do is to go down Times Square or go on a university campus and you see evidences of where this permissiveness has brought us. And you see, the generation gap began this way. The old values of the past generation were based upon the Judeo-Christian concept, the Ten Commandments and the Sermon on the Mount; and the new generation pretty well held to it through grammar school. They began to have their doubts in high school, and they were completely changed by the time they got to college. And so the generation gap by the time a fellow gets his diploma is almost complete between his parents and himself, in what they believe, and what they're committed to.

Now who are these people? Well, first there are the hard-core radicals who talk about the "movement" and the "revolution." A small minority. And then, secondly, there are the idealistic, the "now" generation—they want to remake society, but they don't know how. They believe America is sick, and they're disturbed about poverty and race and war. Then, thirdly, there's another group that are out to rebel just for the heck of it, as they say. And some of them are failures in school, and they want to rationalize their failure by attacking the system. They don't blame themselves; nobody blames himself any more. "It's the system that's wrong. It's somebody in City Hall who's wrong. Somebody in Washington is wrong. *I* couldn't possibly make a mistake." We don't blame ourselves.

And then, fourthly, there's a group that are just plain bored—too much leisure, too much money, no struggle to survive. They have a tendency to blame society for everything. The Bible says the moment that you reach the age of accountability, at about ten years of age or twelve, you're responsible. We are responsible. Of course, society is responsible for many of our terrible social conditions, but for your relationship with God and your personal relationship with your fellow man, the Bible says you're responsible.

You see, many of the books of the Bible were written from prison. You talk about discrimination—Paul had been discriminated against. He was attacked everywhere he went. He finally ended up in prison; but he wrote to the Philippians and said, "Joy, joy, joy. I found nothing but joy in my experience with Christ."

It's possible to live in a rich man's home and be happy. It's possible to live in a ghetto and be happy with Christ in your heart. It's possible to live in a prison, to live in a mental institution, and have Christ in your heart and find peace and happiness.

And then a lot of young people are fed up with paternalism—they're treated like little children, and they want to participate in the decision-making in the university. They rebel against any rigid rules or requirements, even for a bachelor's degree. They don't want to have to take those exams. They don't want to have to do their learning in disciplined study, so sometimes they rebel.

And then they're fed up with hypocrisy. You see, their

parents advocate honesty and integrity and hard work, but they don't see their parents being honest. They don't see integrity in their parents. They don't see their parents really working hard; so they get the wrong set of values, and they see the hypocrisy.

And then they're fed up with irrelevant university and college and high-school teaching, and we have a lot of it today. You see, we've made the mistake of teaching young people how to make a living—only. Now that's fine: learning to make a living—but there's more to life than just bread and butter, and a new car, and a new TV set. Jesus said, "Man shall not live by bread alone." Jesus said, "A man's life consisteth not in the abundance of the things he possesseth." Man is a trinity. He has a mind that needs educating, he has a body that needs medicine and food, but he's a spirit that needs God. He needs a faith; he needs something he can commit himself to. No wonder a university student tore up his diploma the other day in front of thousands of people and said, "My education at this university has been meaningless to me." He learned how to make a living, but he hadn't learned how to live. He hadn't learned how to live and face the problems and the difficulties of life, and he certainly hadn't learned how to die. And I don't think anyone knows how to live till he knows how to die.

And this is where the Gospel of Christ comes in. He forgives the past sin and failure. He gives you a new power now, and He gives you confidence and security and assurance as you face the future.

Now there's something else to all of this, though. The human race automatically rebels. We're all rebels. Adam and Eve rebelled in the Garden of Eden against God. Cain rebelled against the teachings of God and the teachings of his parents, and he killed his brother. The Tower of Babel that you read about in the Bible was nothing but a rebellion. Lot rebelled against Abraham. Esau rebelled against God. He sold his birthright for a bowl of "chili." Seven times in the book of Judges alone the people rebelled, and then under the heat of God's judgment they cried out for a deliverer. Absalom rebelled against David

MAN IN REBELLION

in the Bible. Joshua, the first chapter, the 18th verse, says, "Whosoever he be that doth rebel against thy commandment, and will not hearken unto thy words in all that thou commandest him, he shall be put to death." Job said, "These are those that rebel against the light; they know not the ways thereof, nor abide in the paths thereof." Isaiah, the great prophet of Israel, was speaking of the judgment of God and he said this in the first chapter: "I have nourished and brought up [my] children, and they have rebelled against me."

You see, all the way through the Bible man is rebellious. He's pictured in rebellion against God. We are rebels by nature; and give us half a chance, we'll lash out and we'll fight back at anything around us, like a snake, because we are rebellious. The Bible says, "All have rebelled and come short of the glory of God" because one of the definitions of sin is rebellion. That's how the devil came into existence. Lucifer, son of the morning, rebelled against God in that mysterious past. We don't know much about it, but that's where it all began.

Adam and Eve rebelled against God in the Garden of Eden, and every one of us here is a rebel. We don't want anybody telling us what to do. We don't want God telling us how we ought to live. We don't want God laying out the road to heaven. We want to go some other way. "There is a way that seemeth right unto a man; but the end thereof are the ways of death." The Bible says that the road to heaven is through a narrow gate and a narrow road, and we don't like to be narrow. We think of ourselves as broadminded and tolerant, except in science.

Suppose our men going on Apollo 11 to the moon in July say, "We're way off course." And some men down at Mission Control who are broadminded and tolerant say, "Oh, it's all right. There are many roads that lead to the moon. Just take the one you're on. Any course leads to the moon."

But there are many people who say that about the way to heaven. "Any road will lead you there." Jesus said there's only one road; there's only one way. He said, "I am the way, the truth, and the life: no man cometh unto the Father, but by me."

Now there are thousands of young people here in Madison Square Garden tonight who are searching for purpose and the meaning in their lives. A Columbia University student was quoted two years ago as saying, "America has lost her soul, and we intend to restore it." And the big question at the universities right now is this: "What is the purpose and the meaning of my existence?" Nietzsche once said, "If any man has a 'why' for his life, he can bear with almost any 'how.'" Albert Camus said, "Man cannot live without meaning," and he was right. And many of our modern philosophers from Marcuse on up and down are talking about ultimate situations that we have to face in our lives, and there's nothing we can do about it. "I die; everybody's got to die. I have to face it." "I suffer; everybody suffers. Spiritually, morally, physically, eventually everybody suffers. How do I face suffering?" "I must struggle." "I'm involved and at the mercy of chance." "I have a feeling of guilt." "Who am I?" These are questions that young people are asking everywhere.

And those at the university today—I want to ask you a question. How many scientists at your university consider death a problem to be scientifically studied? How many universities take up the subject of death, suffering, fate, sin, future existence? Modern education has a tendency to avoid and suppress all of these deep questions that students are asking. But the Bible speaks to these questions. The Bible speaks with authority about sin. The Bible speaks with authority about the future life. The Bible speaks with authority as to where you came from and why you're here and where you're going.

There is the problem of God. Tolstoy once said that each of us is stuck with a God-shaped blank. Yes, there is a God. Not out there somewhere, but here. God is everywhere. Throughout the universe He is a person. He is a Spirit. He doesn't have a body like yours and mine; He is Spirit. He can be on Mars at the same time He's on earth. If He had a body like ours, He could only be one place at a time. God is from everlasting to everlasting.

I was talking to Walter Cronkite this past week and we got to talking about space. Did you know that many scientists think that by the end of this century, if the human race lasts that long, we will be able to break the light barrier just as we did the sound barrier? In other words, man will be able to travel at the speed of light. Now when man travels at the speed of light and we go to the nearest star —think of it now—there are billions, and billions, and billions of stars—but should we go to the nearest one, do you know how long it would take the astronauts going at the speed of light to get there? Five years there, five years back, traveling at the speed of light. Now, here's an interesting thing; when they get in the space capsule and leave Cape Kennedy, when they get back, you will be ten years older; I'll be ten years older; but those astronauts will only be ten days older. Why? Because when they break the light barrier, they reach the point where time almost ceases to exist. There is no time in space. No yesterday, no tomorrow; and it took science in 1969 to find out something the Bible has taught all along. God is from everlasting to everlasting. There is no future with God, no past with God, everything is in the eternal present with God. "A day with the Lord is as a thousand years, and a thousand years as a day."

Ah, yes, God is. Do you believe that? The first step is to believe Him.

And then the second problem is the problem of man. One of our famous writers said there's no meaning to anything in life. Eugene O'Neill once said, "Life's only meaning is death." And you know, students, I find everywhere, feel as though they're IBM cards. They're just numbers. This is one of the problems in the educational system today. There's no personal interaction and relationship between students and faculty. They've become just numbers. And many students live in a state of spiritual nihilism. Now nihilism believes nothing—no morality, no purpose, no meaning for anything; and there are many like that today. But the Bible teaches that God has a purpose for the human race. God created us in His image, and you as a person are important to God. The Bible says that God has the hairs of your head numbered. The Bible says that God watches you from the moment of conception, in your mother's womb, the moment of birth; every moment of your life is watched by God. He watches the moment of your death. Everything is held and accounted for. He knows all the moral choices you have; He knows all the options you have. For example, when you are immoral, when you tell a lie—He knows the options you had. You could have told the truth. There was a way of escape from that immorality, like Joseph escaping from Potiphar's wife, but you didn't take it. It's all on God's computers so that at the judgment nobody's going to say, "God, You're unjust." He knows all the factors that went into your life, and it will all be properly evaluated and weighed; and you'll never be able to say, "God, You weren't just."

And then there's the problem of human iniquity. What causes greed and lust and prejudice and war? We're wrestling with a race problem in the United States. We're wrestling with a crime problem. We're wrestling with a war problem. We're wrestling with a poverty problem. Where did all that come from? In 2 Thessalonians, the Scripture says, "For the mystery of iniquity doth already work." There's a mystery to it. It's a spirit. There's a spirit of evil at work in our world, and don't ever forget it. There is God, but there is also the spirit of evil—the devil. You can call him any name you like. There is a power of evil in this world, and you cannot explain all the evil that is going on in our world today unless you understand there is a supernatural force back of it called the devil that Jesus referred to time after time. Yes, the Bible says it comes out of our hearts. For Jesus said, "For out of the heart proceed evil thoughts and murders and adulteries and fornications and thefts and false witness and blasphemies."

John Lennon, the Beatle, said in Canada the other day a very interesting thing as quoted in the press. He said, "If sin means missing the mark, then I'm a sinner." John

Lennon's right. He is a sinner. So am I. So are you, because sin is missing God's standard and God's requirements for us. We have come short; we need reconciliation. We need forgiveness. And that's why Christ came and died on the Cross.

And then there's the problem of guilt that a lot of young people wrestle with. A Radcliffe girl was quoted in *Time* magazine as saying, "I always feel guilty." Where does it come from? Is there a universal moral law after all? Psychology has recognized the centrality of guilt. God says, "I have written my law in your heart."

You know, one of the great psychologists of this country was quoted some time ago—and I haven't had a chance to check this quote, but I'm going to give it to you —and he said 95 percent of the insanity of this country was caused by the fact that the victim at some crucial stage in the journey of life refused forgiveness of sin. Everybody wants to be forgiven. We all know we've sinned. We all know we've failed, but do you know you're forgiven? Well, that's why Christ came. That's why He died on the Cross.

Goethe, the great German philosopher, once said, "If I were God, this world of sin and suffering would break my heart." Well, I want to tell you, it did break God's heart; and that's why Christ died on the Cross. That's why He shed His blood, because God took your sins, and my sins, and put them on Christ; and He became "sin for us, who knew no sin." You can be forgiven. Your sins can be wiped away.

Then you face the problem of suffering; and you can say with the apostle, "For our light affliction, which is but for a moment, worketh for a far more exceeding and eternal weight of glory." You can face the problem of death. The Bible says there is "a time to be born and a time to die." Paul said, "I have fought a good fight . . . I am now ready to be offered up. To die is gain." Wilhelm Stekel said, "Every fear we have is ultimately the fear of death." The Bible says God did not create man to die. The Scripture says that Christ "hath abolished death, and hath brought life and immortality to light through the gospel." Christian faith is a resurrection faith. The fear of death is removed when you give your life to Christ.

Oh, yes, there'll be an uneasiness. There's always a tension about the unknown; but when you receive Christ, the sting of death is gone. You can look at life with a clear eye, a spring in your step, and a smile on your face because your past is forgiven. You know you're here, created in God's image to glorify God. You know where you're going. You're going to spend eternity with Christ. You can say, "O Death, where is thy sting?"

That's the flag I'm asking you to follow. That's what I'm asking you to believe. That's what I'm asking you to commit yourself to. We've seen these marvelous men and women of the Salvation Army here tonight, and we're honored to have General Coutts with us. These people have a cause; they take a cup of cold water in one hand; social activism of the highest order. They actually go out and help people in need, but in the other hand, they also carry the love of Christ. They carry the Gospel of the Lord Jesus Christ.

Tonight America and the world needs young people who will march under the banner of Jesus Christ. You'll not be ashamed of Him. You will take your stand for Him at all times. You're willing to be laughed at and persecuted. You're willing for your friends to sneer at you and call you a "square" or call you other names. But tonight you're ready to commit your life to Him and follow Him and serve Him and enlist in His army and say tonight, "I want to go out with love in my heart. I want to go out and help change my world by changing men. I'm willing to follow Christ and serve Christ, whatever the cost." And it'll cost you something, because I have something to tell you. It's not easy to be a Christian. It's not easy to follow Christ. In the world in which we're living with the materialistic pressures, secularistic pressures, the sensual pressures, it's not easy to live clean and pure before God; but you can with Christ's help.

And I'm asking you tonight to receive Him. You say, "Billy, what do I have to do?" First of all, you have to repent of your sin. That means that you're willing to turn from your sin; it means that you're willing to acknowledge that you've sinned. Are you willing to do that? That's repentance. Secondly, by faith you receive Jesus Christ as your Lord, your Master, and your Savior. "If we confess with our mouths the Lord Jesus and believe in our hearts that God hath raised Him from the dead, we shall be saved."

I'm asking you to do it publicly. Why publicly? Jesus said, "If you're not willing to acknowledge me before men, I'll not acknowledge you before my Father which is in heaven." There's something about coming publicly that settles it in your heart. When you got married, you got married in front of witnesses. When you come to Christ, you come openly and take your stand for Him. You may be a member of the church; you may not be a member of any church. You may be Catholic or Protestant or Jewish or Moslem, or you may not have any religion. But you want to come tonight and commit your life to Christ and receive Him as your Savior and trust Him.

I'm going to ask you to come. I'm going to ask you to get up out of these seats all over this great stadium and come and stand in front of this platform quietly and reverently. And after you've all come here, I'm going to say a word to you, have a prayer with you, and give you some literature. A counselor will say a word to you. Then you can go back and join your friends. If you've come with friends or relatives or in a bus, they'll wait on you. I'm going to ask you to come. Right now. Men, women, young people, from all over this stadium. Up in the balcony, those who have to come from that top gallery, you have to go out and around and come down. But all of you others can come straight down on the floor right now. And then those of you that are watching by closed-circuit television at the Manhattan Center, you can receive Christ right where you are by getting up out of your seats and coming to Christ.

All of you who are watching by television, I do not know whether you can see this great sight of hundreds of people coming from every direction here at the Madison Square Garden to give their lives and their hearts to

Christ. Where you are in your home or wherever you happen to be, you can make your commitment to Christ in your heart right now.

Delivered June 15, 1969

IV.

THE PRODIGAL SON

Now tonight, let's turn to the 15th chapter of Luke. I'm not going to read the passage because it's too long, but it is a familiar story that all of us have read and heard since childhood. It is called "The Story of the Prodigal Son." That's what we call it. There are many ways we could term this passage from Luke's Gospel. It could be called "The Story of the Loving Father." It could be called "The Story of the Church Member Without Christ," because that is exactly what the elder brother was.

But tonight I want to dwell on the story of this boy because he was a rebel. He rebelled against his father. And you know what I read the other day? That over two thousand young people who run away from home come to New York every month seeking fame and fortune. They become prey to all the thugs and con-men and drug merchants and sex perverts and all the others. Two thousand a month are lured away from their parents to New York City.

This is also a city where young people do a lot of damage. Do you know last year how many school windows were broken in New York? Over 200,000. Do you know how many telephone booths were wrecked in the city of New York last year? Over 300,000. And did you know that these crimes are largely among young people? Now I grant you the older people tell them how to do it, and it is

THE PRODIGAL SON

the older people who print the pornography, and it is the older people who produce the motion pictures, and it is the older people who think up all the violence on television, and it is the older people who have handed this world and the mess we're in to our young people.

But young people are striking out at society in every kind of way today. Some of it is violent, some is destructive, some of it is just plain rebellion, and some of it is justified.

This is the story of a young fellow who ran away from home. Now in this passage Jesus tells three little stories. Jesus always used stories to illustrate spiritual truths. They are called parables in the Bible. He told a story of a lost sheep. He told a story of a lost coin. He told a story of this lost son, and in all three stories he is picturing a loving father searching for that which is lost, and that Father is God. You see God is searching for you tonight. God loves you. He is searching for you, and the search takes Him all the way to the Cross where He gives His Son for you. That is how much God loves you.

But it is also a story of how we are lost from God. The Bible teaches that we are like the lost sheep or the lost coin or the lost boy. We are away from God. We have rebelled against God. We have run away from God, but God loves us. He wants us back, and He is willing to go to any length to get us back. He won't compromise in telling us how to get back. Some people try to come other ways. He said, "There is only one way back and that is by the Cross. There is only one way back and that's through my Son, Jesus Christ. If you are willing to come that way I will receive you and I will forgive you." And that's the story of this boy. One day he goes to his father and says, "Dad, you know I am tired of living out here in the country—all the discipline and the hard work—and I am eighteen years of age. I would like to have my inheritance now and I want to go out to 'New York' because I am going to make it big up there." He had read about "Broadway" and he had heard all about the bright lights. He had heard about all the different things that happened there, and he decided he would like to go.

And his father said, "Son, I don't advise it, but if you are determined to go, go ahead." And so he starts out for the big city.

You know this weekend one of the people who made the news all across the country was a brilliant young member of the senior class at Wellesley. She expressed how young people are feeling lost today. She described how young people are exploring a world that none of us understand, and are searching for more immediate and static and penetrating modes of living. And what she was saying was this: young people are lost, confused and frustrated and are searching for a way back.

And this is what Jesus Himself said. He said, "The Son of Man is come to seek and save that which is lost."

Well, this young fellow came from an affluent home. They had a great deal of love in the home, a great deal of discipline in the home, and there was faith in God. I imagine his father gathered the family together every day for prayer and Bible reading, and the boy said, "Oh, I don't want to talk about God. I don't want religion. I can't wait to get away from home."

How many young people are like that here tonight?

Or, maybe he had to go to church. And he said, "I don't want to go to church. I can't wait until I can get away and get to the university and get to college, and go to town—get somewhere so I don't have to get to church."

So he rebelled against his father, and rebellion became a way of life for him.

Now it is perfectly normal for a young fellow to pull away from his father. The Bible says, "Therefore shall a man leave his father and mother and cleave unto his wife and they shall be one flesh." After you are married you are in for trouble if you start living with your parents and depending on your parents. Live with your wife; be on your own; establish your own friends. But here was a young man in his teens, not married, and the reason he was leaving home was because he didn't like the discipline at home. He wanted to go out and have a good time. Now if he wanted to go out and work and get a job, that was one thing, but that wasn't what he wanted. He wanted to "goof off." He didn't want to go to school any more. He didn't want to get up and milk the cows on the farm any more. He wanted to go out and have a good time. It was to please self.

You know down here on Times Square—I've walked down there a couple of times, and one of those theaters down there has a big marquee that says, "Unsatisfied." And then you know the pop song that the Rolling Stones made so famous, "I Can't Get No Satisfaction"?

Well, this young fellow was going out trying to find fulfillment and satisfaction and happiness, and he thought it lay where all the bright lights and the music and the night clubs and all the rest were. He said, "I am going to have a real ball."

I heard about a girl the other day. She was wooed by a boy with promises of marriage. She became pregnant. He left her alone. Her father, mother and family suffered shame and disgrace because of a boy's selfishness, and that is the very essence of sin—selfishness. That is what sin is all about—self. I want to satisfy self.

I was interviewed on television by a group of students this past week, and one of them said, "What is wrong with being aroused sexually?" He said, "I go out and buy my sex. What's wrong with that?" Well, the thing that is wrong with it is that the ingredient that sex was made for is not there—love within marriage. Some go out and buy it like shopping in a supermarket—like a steak, like a lunch—with no love, no relationship.

The Bible goes further. It says it is wrong outside of marriage.

But you see this boy was already wandering away from home even while he was at home. He was thinking about it. We don't wander away all at once. Like sheep, we wander gradually. The Bible says, "All we like sheep have gone astray." And so this young fellow went, and when he got to town he was like the fellow I read about in London, England, in one of the British newspapers, who had a home in the country and a home in town. He said, "When I am in the country, I want to be in the city, and when I am in the city, I want to be in the country." The problem was not where he was; the problem was his own heart. Going to town is not going to meet your needs. Going to the country is not going to meet your needs.

I talked to a young person day before yesterday, and he said, "Boy, I'd like to get out of this rat race in this city and get out to the country and listen to the birds and see the grass." Well, he'd be out there about three days and he'd be wanting to hear the honking of the taxicabs and hear all the screaming of the sirens.

You see it is a heart problem we have. We want fulfillment in our lives. We want a peace and a joy and a happiness that we don't find anywhere in life. It is just not found apart from God. You can't find it just anywhere.

And during this past week I have been very interested in reading some of the addresses being given by valedictorians and professors and famous people at the various universities and colleges. Nearly all of them were pessimistic. Every one of them said that young people were looking for something they can't find, and the youth themselves, I thought, brought the greatest message. They said, "We are living in a lousy, messed up world. We feel lousy ourselves. We don't know the answer." And it was very pessimistic, this commencement season across the country. And one young fellow got up and told them. He said, "This university is standing now, but we're going to be back. We're going to be back this fall and we're going to burn it down." That's how he felt.

I talked to a fellow the other day right here in New York City. He said, "Yes, we're going to burn the town down." I said, "What are you going to build in its place?" He said, "Oh, we don't have any plans for that, but anything is better than what we've got now. We are going to tear it down."

Well, I agree there are a lot of things wrong. A lot of things need straightening out, but I don't believe the way to do it is to tear it down and burn it up. Let's try to use the democratic processes and straighten it out because I'm not so sure that some of the people I've seen marching around saying they are going to change it all would do any better than the people who are running it now. They don't seem to have any ideas—any constructive ideas.

But you see, this fellow went off to town, and when he got there he had his pockets full of money. Well, anyone who has any money has a crowd around him. You can make friends quickly if you've got money. I would hate to be a wealthy man because I would never know who my friends were. Everybody is after your money. When your money is gone your friends are gone. Some friends are free loaders. His friends were. He had a lot of friends around him.

Did you read the other day in the paper that in the Detroit Zoo they lost their prize ostrich? I think her name was Susie, and they performed an autopsy on Susie and found $3.85 in pennies, dimes and quarters inside that beautiful bird. That bird was killed by money.

This fellow had a lot of money—went off to town, and got a lot of friends around him. The Bible says there is pleasure in sin. He started doing the things that he learned from his city cousins. He learned a little bit about dope. He took some "trips." At first it was just a lot of fun, a lot of kicks. It wasn't long until he began to be hooked. He started taking a few sips of alcohol and it wasn't long before he had to have it before lunch. He began to fool around with a girl. It wasn't long before he was in trouble—had to move to the other side of town. All kinds of trouble plagued him.

You see the devil is fishing with bait. He comes along and whispers in your ear and tells you that it is greener on the other side of the fence. Everything is better over there. You just rebel against your parents, rebel against God, rebel against religion, and go out here on your own and you think it's going to be better. But the devil doesn't tell you that he's got a hook in you. Fools make a mockery of sin. The Bible says, "Be sure your sin will find you out." The Bible says, "There is pleasure in sin for a season." You see, for a short time you can have a good time, but it is very short. It disappears. It becomes empty. You become disillusioned! Disenchanted!

I was in a European country last summer, and one of

the top young people told me—he said, "You know, we've had this permissive society now for a generation." And he said, "Anything goes and we are filled up to here with it. We are sick of it. Let's take a walk down through the streets of Stockholm." He said, "Do you see much laughter, much joy, much happiness?" There were throngs of young people, but there was something missing. They looked bored. They had one of the highest suicide rates among young people in the world. Why? Because all of this permissiveness without discipline doesn't bring happiness. Happiness and peace and joy are found in God, in a relationship with Jesus Christ, and in a disciplined life.

The Bible says, "Sin when it is finished bringeth forth death."

And the Bible says that this young fellow began to be in want. It wasn't long before his money was gone; he spent it all. And when his money left him, his friends left him.

I read the other day in the *Daily News*—I think they called it "The Prodigal Daughter." She was nineteen years of age, she had a steady boyfriend to whom she was engaged until one day she stepped out on him. She was unfaithful to him, and listen to what she says as quoted:

"I got into trouble with a guy I don't even like because I went to a drug and booze party. I completely lost control of myself, and I didn't even know what happened except that the guy whose baby I am going to have disappeared after he heard of my condition. I brought shame to my family and friends, and now I cry myself to sleep at night. I feel like I am falling apart. I haven't gone out of the house since it happened."

She began to be in want. She went to a party to have a big time, but there came a moment when sin paid its wages. And it always does. You see you can't commit a single sin without paying for it. You may not pay for it immediately. You may not pay for it as quickly as this girl, but you're going to pay for it.

The Bible says, "Whatsoever a man soweth that shall he also reap."

This young man began to be in want.

There is a film in New York for "Adults Only," and it is entitled, "I Want."

The Bible says, "The Lord is my shepherd, I shall not want."

But you see, the Lord was not the shepherd of this boy. He began to be in want. His body began to be in want. Is your body in want tonight for bigger kicks, more high-powered drugs, more sex deviation to satisfy—trying to stay awake at night thinking up things you can do for kicks? Is your mind in want?

The Bible says our minds have been affected by sin and the more we learn, the less truth we know many times— "ever learning but never able to come to a knowledge of truth," because, you see, God is Truth, Christ is Truth, and if you don't know Christ, you don't have the foundation of truth.

And, so many of our scientists today—see how many breakthroughs we have. They are beginning to see new areas of knowledge they didn't know existed a few years ago. Knowledge is now doubling every ten years so that no scientist can know it all. They can only specialize in one small field, and a scientist feels frustrated and hemmed in.

Dr. Elmer Engstrom, who spoke to you a moment ago, Chairman of this Crusade, is a great scientist, and he would tell you that scientists feel frustrated because they have to specialize now in little fields, and they cannot have the whole range of knowledge they once had.

And you see, the spirit began to be in want. He rebelled against God. The human soul is so large the world cannot satisfy it. "What shall it profit a man if he gain the whole world and lose his own soul."

And then something interesting happened. He became a slave. He had to find employment, but a depression had come, and he couldn't get a job. Finally, the only job he could get was to go out and feed the hogs. And so Jesus said he went out and began to feed the swine. And then he became so hungry that he began to eat with the hogs. It wasn't long before he looked like a hog. He smelled like a hog. He grunted like a hog. Down in the pigpen with the hogs—a boy who had come from a fine home—gone to have a big time in the big city. How many in New York are like that tonight? Or any of the other great cities of America? In rebellion, going into all kinds of sin, but becoming slaves of sin. Jesus said, "Whoever committeth sin is the slave of sin."

He had walked out on his father and the love and the discipline of his father, to come under the bondage of a stranger. What an exchange! "What shall a man give in exchange for his soul?"

You know Prince Philip was speaking a few days ago at Edinburgh, and he said something I like. He got pretty tough with some students. He said, "Shut up and grow up." He said, "Freedom is not license. You can destroy freedom as successfully by making a mockery of it as you can by retraction." Hurray for Prince Philip! Maybe he will become an evangelist yet.

The Bible says that we cannot be neutral. Lots of people try to be neutral. They say, "Well, I'm not for God, I'm not against Him. I just don't take a stand." But God says you have to take a stand. You have to choose—you have to choose which road of life you are going to go—a broad road or a narrow road. The narrow road leads to heaven, the broad road leads to hell, and you must make the choice.

And so this young fellow got to thinking one day, and it's a good thing when you start to think about yourself. He began to think, and the Spirit of God began to speak to him, and he began to think about his father back there on the farm. He thought to himself, "What am I doing here in these rags, in this dirt, in this filth, eating with hogs when my father has a beautiful farm back there with many servants and many cattle, and I could go be there and be a servant of his. What a fool I've made of myself."

You know the Bible teaches that sin is a form of insanity? The Bible says if our Gospel is hid or veiled, the veil must be in the minds of those who have spiritually died. The spirit of this world has blinded the minds of those who do not believe and who prevent the light of the glorious Gospel of Christ, the image of God, from shining in there. Notice, "The spirit of this world." There is an evil spirit in our world that blinds us to the reality of what God can do. It blinds us to our own condition. Then the Holy Spirit comes along and convinces us and disturbs us of our sins, and we sit and think about it and we are disturbed and unhappy about our condition. We don't know where to escape. We don't know which way to go. But this young fellow decided to do the right thing. He decided to get up and go back. He said, "I have sinned against heaven." He didn't just say, "I have sinned against my father." He said, "I have sinned against God." That's your problem. Your problem is not a family relationship. Your problem is not really a race problem. Your problem is a problem with God. You get the problem with God straightened out, and you will have a new perspective on how to straighten out some of the other problems. That's the real problem. The real hangup in your life is what to do about God, what to do about Christ. Let Him come and change and transform your life and see the fulfillment and the power and the strength you will have.

This young fellow reflected; then he made a resolution. He said, "I will arise and go to my father."

Sixteen thousand young people in Miami the other day arose and demonstrated for decency. Thousands of young people followed an Olympic track star down the streets of Toronto the other day, to witness for Christ. They called it "A mile for morals march." When are we going to wake up? When are the young people in this country who believe in God finally going to start carrying their flag? Maybe we are going to see a great tide turned, but we will never turn unless we are willing to make Christ the very heart and the very center of our lives. There is nothing else in the arena of American philosophy and thought today except Christ. It is either Christ or it is chaos. Which is it going to be?

The Beatles' latest controversial record is called, "Oh, Christ, It Ain't Easy," and it's not easy to follow Christ. It is not easy to be a Christian. It's not easy to live in New York or any of our other great metropolitan areas and live the disciplined life for Jesus Christ. It's not easy for a young person to resist the temptations of this hour.

Jesus said, "Sit down and count the cost. If you want something easy, then go somewhere else. I'm not the man; I'm not the one." He said, "Count the cost." He said, "It's going to mean death to self—your own self-interests, your own self-pride." He said, "It's going to mean a cross. You may have to be crucified." He meant that not only figuratively; He also meant it literally. It is going to have to mean less of you and your desires and your ambitions, and Christ is going to have to be first, and He'll test you; He'll take you to many Crosses, and He will see if you are willing to go there without flinching. That is what it will cost to follow Christ.

This fellow said, "I will arise and go."

He started back home, and while he was a long way off, his father was watching for him. Now notice, this is a picture of God. Jesus is telling a story to illustrate a spiritual truth. Here is a picture of God watching you all the time. He sees you coming down the road, and the son is filled with shame, and dirt, and filth, and sin, and rebellion. Was his father apathetic to his condition? Was his father indifferent? No. The Bible says that he was watching, waiting for his son to return, hoping and praying he would return. And when he saw him, he ran down the road and threw his arms around him and the son blurted out in tears, "Father, I have sinned against you. I am sorry. I have come home to be a servant."

But the father said, "Nothing doing." He said, "Bring the ring and put it on his finger, the ring of the authority of sonship. Give him a bath and put on the finest clothes, and then kill the fatted calf. We are going to have a barbecue, we're going to have a party that will be the greatest party we ever had. My son that was lost has been found. My son has returned." The Bible says, "There is rejoicing in heaven over one sinner that repents." That is why Madison Square Garden is worth all the expense and all the trouble and all the work if just one person comes to Christ. If you know the value of one soul, if you knew it made heaven rejoice over one person returning to the Father, you would receive Christ. You would return to the Father. You say, "But Billy, you don't know my sins. You don't know how rebellious my heart has been. You don't know how many lies I've told, how many immoralities I've committed, how many drugs I've taken. You don't know all I've done. I couldn't possibly come."

You are the kind of person He is really looking for. He receives you tonight. Jesus receives sinful men. That's why He died. That's why He rose again—to receive you.

But then out in the field there was his brother. He hadn't seen his younger brother for years. He was working out in the fields and he heard all the shouting and all the commotion, and he said, "What's going on?" One of the servants said, "Your brother has returned." He said, "That scoundrel? You mean that reprobate, that sinner has returned and he expects us to welcome him?"

You see this fellow had been in his father's home all along, but his loyalty wasn't really to his father. His loyalty was to his own selfish interests. And it is possible to be in the church and be lost. It is possible to be in the church and be without a personal relationship with Jesus Christ. And there is many an elder brother here tonight. You are a member of the church, you haven't yet left home, but even while you are at home, in the church, your heart is not right with God. You need to repent of your sins and receive Christ as your Lord and as your Savior.

Lincoln—before he was killed—was asked how he would treat the rebellious Southerners, and he answered "As if they had never been away." That is how God will treat you if you receive Christ tonight—as if you had never been away. He forgives all the past. He writes your name in His book. You have the assurance that you are going to heaven. Now it is complicated, and it is hard to live the Christian life. I don't want to fool you. I don't want you to come under false colors. It is not easy to be a Christian. It means reading your Bible daily, it means spending time in prayer, and it means persecution.

"All that will live godly in Christ Jesus shall suffer persecution," the Bible says.

We are to live disciplined lives, under the Lordship of Christ. That is not easy, but let me tell you something. The Holy Spirit comes to live in your heart to help you live the Christian life, and then He begins to live through you and in you. It is no longer you living. It is Christ living in you, and it becomes a life of joy. Problems? Yes. Difficulties? Yes. But a life of joy and peace and forgiveness. He can change your life tonight.

There is a man here in this audience whom I saw here a moment ago. Maybe you saw me put my arm around him when I came into the Garden. His name is Jim Vaus. Jim does one of the great social jobs here in New York City. Twenty years ago this year, Jim wandered into a tent where we were holding a meeting in Los Angeles. Jim—he wouldn't mind me saying this—was Mickey Cohen's wire tapper, had been written up as one of the great criminals of the West Coast. That night Jim found Christ. He and Alice with their children are here tonight, love the Lord with all their heart, and Jim speaks all over the world. Thousands of people have found Christ under his ministry. What Christ has done for Jim Vaus He can do for you tonight if you put your faith and your confidence in Him. I am going to ask you to do it tonight. You ask, "What do I have to do, Billy?"

I am going to ask you to get up and come.

Delivered June 16, 1969

V.

HEAVEN AND HELL

I am going to ask that we bow our heads in prayer. Every head bowed and every eye closed. People are here from various parts of the United States and, for that matter, the world. We represent various nationalities; many of us speak with accents because we have come from abroad to be here in New York City, to live here, to work here. Or perhaps you are a tourist visiting here. Whoever you are, there is one thing we all have in common: Our hearts are the same. Whatever the color of the skin, or whatever the accent we speak with, our hearts are the same—the same fears, the same longings, the same sins—troubles, problems, difficulties. Well, I tell you tonight Christ can help you. He can take the guilt away, and He can give you a joy, a peace and a new dimension of living, if you let Him. And I am going to ask you to listen very quietly and very prayerfully tonight. My message will be brief.

"Our Father and our God we pray that Thy Holy Spirit will speak to us and draw us to the Savior. For we ask it in His Name, Amen."

Now tonight I want you to turn with me to two passages of Scripture, the last part of the 23rd Psalm that was read a few moments ago—The words of David as a Shepherd:

". . . and I will dwell in the house of the Lord for ever."

Now most of the creeds of the church teach life after death.

I want to talk tonight about the future life and the choice we must make now. Now this is an election day in New York City, and you do a strange thing here that I have not seen before. The election polls did not open until 3:00 and they closed at 10:00. I think I've got that right if I read the paper correctly. And usually it is sunrise to sunset down where I live, and we thought that tonight most of our people would be away voting. Apparently, the vote must have been light because I think most of you came here. The Garden is not only packed, but people are in the overflow auditorium in the beautiful Forum watching by closed-circuit television. Lee Fisher, one of my associates, told me a little story today about Al Smith when he was Governor of New York. He went to speak at Sing Sing. He had never spoken to inmates in a prison before, and he didn't know how to start. He was a little bit embarrassed and he started out by saying, "My fellow citizens," and then he thought to himself, "Well, they've lost their citizenship." So, he cleared his throat and started over and said, "My fellow convicts." And that didn't sound exactly right, so he backed up and started over again. He said, "Well, anyway, I'm glad to see so many of you here." Politics haven't changed very much.

But the second passage of Scripture has something to do about choice. It's from the Sermon on the Mount, and it's the words of our Lord in the 7th chapter, in which He says,

"Enter ye in at the strait gate: for wide is the
gate, and broad is the way, that leadeth to destruction, and many there be which go in thereat:
Because strait is the gate, and narrow is the
way, which leadeth unto life, and few . . ."

Notice our Lord said "few there be that find it."

Jesus Christ taught that there are two roads of life. He taught there are two masters. You are either mastered by self or you are mastered by God, and He said you cannot serve both at the same time.

And He said that there are two destinies, heaven and hell.

Now Christ doesn't divide men between black and white, rich or poor, or educated and uneducated. He divides us into two classes—those who are on the broad road that leads to destruction and those on the narrow road that leads to eternal life. Which road are you on?

You know we don't hear much preaching on the subject of the after-life any more. How long has it been since you heard a sermon on hell or heaven?

You know Winston Churchill said a few years ago, "The moral landslide in Great Britain can be traced to the fact that heaven and hell are no longer proclaimed throughout the land."

In an article some time ago, in an editorial, a major news magazine pleaded for more Hell preaching.

You know somehow we have planned everything as though this life is the sum total of our existence. The Bible teaches that this life is only a preparation for eternity. Our lives will go on for millions and millions of years. And the choice we make now decides the type of life we are going to live in the future. Now we may not like that. I know that kind of talk today is not popular.

But Jesus said, "A man's life consisteth not in the abundance of the things he possesses." Jesus taught "that man shall not live by bread alone." But we are trying to prove that if we have a high standard of living and can somehow make it to a good retirement, we are all right. But the Bible teaches that we are a mind; we need education. We are a body; we need medicine, we need food, we need drink. But we are also a spirit, and the spirit of man is going to live forever. The "real you" that lives inside your body is destined for eternity. God has put eternity in our hearts, said King Solomon many centuries ago.

Now Jesus said, "There is a broad road of life, and it is the road that leads to destruction." Many of you are on that road tonight. The extremes of humanity are there— the sex glutton, the dope pusher, the murderer, the rapist, the mugger—but a lot of church people, too. Over on the next page in the same chapter in the Sermon on the Mount, there were people who thought they were going to get to heaven, and when they got there Jesus said, "I don't even know you."

"But, Lord, I cast out demons in your name. Lord, I was an evangelist. Lord, I was this; I was that."

Jesus is going to say, "I didn't even know you."

This broad road that leads to destruction is a *deceptive road*. "There is a way that seemeth right unto a man, but the end thereof is a way of death."

You see, it seems right to live for self. It seems right to live a selfish life and get what you can get out of life, for your own pleasures, your own appetite. But the end is death, says the Bible. We need to spend some more time thinking about the future and what the future holds.

And then Jesus said, "Not only is it a deceptive road, but it *leads to hell*."

Now I know you don't hear much preaching about it, but everybody else is using the word "Hell." We use it on television now; we use it in the movies. Many of our major motion pictures use the word "Hell." There is a film showing right now called *Hell's Cat*. And the film industry has been using it for years. Remember *Hell's Angels, To Hell and Back, The City of Hell, Hell's Return, Hell Bent for Glory, Hell and High Water, The Wicked Go to Hell*—every kind of motion picture using the word "Hell." And I hear the word "Hell" used all the time—in elevators, in airplanes, and wherever I am traveling—in hotels. I never hear the word "heaven." Why doesn't a fellow say, "To heaven with you"? You never hear that!

You know, I asked a psychiatrist friend of mine about this some time ago, and you know he had an interesting answer. He said, "Something deep inside of our subconscious makes us afraid that we may go to hell, and so we use the word "hell" all the time."

Now the Bible has a lot to say about it. Jesus had a lot to say about it. He talked about it a number of times. In fact He talked about it more than anybody else. And He said that Hell was not prepared for man. God never meant that man would ever go to Hell. Hell was prepared for the devil and his angels, but man rebelled against God and followed the devil. And the existence of Hell indicates that man has freedom of choice. You have a choice —the broad road, or the narrow road, and at the end of the broad road is a place or a condition that Jesus described as Hell. At the end of the narrow road is a place or a condition that Jesus described as Heaven, and every one of us is on one road or the other, leading to those two destinies.

Now the Bible teaches there is a judgment. "God will bring every deed into judgment with every secret thing whether good or evil."

The Psalmist said, "God will judge the world with righteousness and the peoples by his truth."

And the Apostle Paul wrote to the Thessalonians and said, "When the Lord Jesus shall be revealed from heaven with his mighty angels in flaming fire taking vengeance on them that know not God, and that obey not the Gospel of our Lord Jesus Christ, who shall be punished with everlasting destruction from the presence of the Lord and from the glory of His power."

Now what does that mean? What do all of those passages mean? Whatever Hell may be, and there are many mysteries, and I don't intend to solve them all—whatever Hell may mean, it is separation from God.

Now there are *three words* that Jesus used constantly to describe it. One is called *"Fire."* Now we know that God has a fire that burns and doesn't consume like the burning bush that Moses experienced. We know that James said, "The tongue is set on fire of hell." We know that that wasn't combustion—that actual literal fire isn't down in your throat and in your tongue. It is symbolic language. And theologians through the centuries have argued and debated over what fire means.

The Bible said, "For our God is a consuming fire."

Jesus told the story about the rich man who went to Hell and he asked that Lazarus may dip the tip of his finger in water and cool his tongue.

Could it be that the fire Jesus talked about is an eternal search for God that is never quenched? Is that what it means? That, indeed, would be hell. To be away from God forever, separated from His Presence.

Jesus said, "I am the water of life," and never to know the water of life would be hell.

And then He used another word. He used the word *"darkness."* Now the Bible says, "God is light." And Jesus said, "The children of the Kingdom shall be cast into outer darkness."

He said in Matthew 22, "Bind him hand and foot and take him away and cast him into outer darkness."

The Apostle Peter said, "God spared not the angels that sin but cast them into hell and delivered them into chains of darkness."

What does that mean? There again, the darkness is separation from God. God is light. Separation from light is darkness.

And then the *third word* that Jesus used is *death—the second death* in the Bible. God is life. Hell is death to the spirit, death to the soul, separation from God, "Death and hell were cast into the lake of fire." This is the second death, says the Scripture.

Now the Bible teaches that God does not take any delight in this. God loves you. He sent His Son to keep you from being lost. He sent the Holy Spirit to prompt you and convince you so that you would not be lost. And if you are lost, and if you go to Hell, it will be by your own deliberate choice, because God never meant that you go there. It is your own decision. Now that is a terrifying thought, and it should disturb all of us.

You say, "Well, Billy, I'm not sure I can accept that." I know that according to the latest national poll, sixty-five percent of Americans believe there is a Hell. Thirty-five percent say there is none. Well, let's just suppose there is a ten percent chance that Jesus was right. Just a ten percent chance. Let's say there is a ten percent chance that there is an after-life and that there is a life of destruction and separation from God. I want to ask you, "Is it worth taking that chance?" If I went out to Kennedy Airport and they told me, "There is a ten percent chance this plane you are going to get on is not going to make it. We found out there is something wrong with the motor; but we are going anyway."

I tell you, I'm going to wait for a later plane!

And yet how many of us take a chance on our lives, our eternal souls. You have a choice.

Yes, there is the broad road. Jesus said many are on that road. The majority of humanity is on that road. "Many there are which go in thereat."

But now let's come to the *narrow road*. Only a few are on that road. Jesus said, "Few there be that go in thereat." Jesus said, "The entrance to that road is a narrow gate." Notice, "a narrow gate." Now we don't like that word "narrow." We are living in an age of tolerance. We are living in an age when "every man is for himself. You can believe anything you want to believe."

You know, it's not true in most realms of life.

Suppose those astronauts who are going to go to the moon in July get on the wrong path and in the wrong orbit, and the people in Houston say, "Oh, that's all right.

There are a number of roads leading up there. Keep going." They would keep going; never be back. No, they go by precise laws. All of nature is run by precise laws. We know at what temperature water boils. We know at what temperature water freezes. We know all of these scientific laws work in perfect precision. We are discovering the laws of nature.

Why would God be haphazard about spiritual and moral laws? They are just as precise, if not more so. Jesus said, "The road is narrow; the gate is narrow." And He said, "If you're going to go the narrow road that leads to eternal life, you'll have to go through the narrow gate." Now, what is that gate? Jesus said, "I am the way. I am the door. By me if any man enter in he shall be saved." Jesus said, "Don't try to come some other way. That's like a robber." He said, "There is only one door. There is only one gate. I am the way. I am the truth. I am the light. I am the way to Heaven. You have to come by Me."

Now you say, "Billy, I can't accept that. I want to go to Heaven. I've got a feeling there is an after-life, and I've got a feeling that maybe there is a Heaven, but I just don't want to come by the way of Jesus."

Well, I am sorry, but I cannot compromise at that point. I have to go by the rule book. I cannot bargain. I have no authority from the Bible to bargain with your soul. I have no authority to lower the standards. Jesus said, "I am the door. By me if any man enter in he shall be saved."

Jesus said, "Except your righteousness exceed the righteousness of the Scribes and Pharisees, ye shall in no wise enter into heaven."

The righteousness He requires is beyond works. You cannot work your way to heaven and you cannot buy your way to heaven. It is a gift of God because of what Christ did on the Cross.

"So by grace are ye saved, through faith, and that not of yourself. It is a gift of God, not of works lest any man should boast."

You say, "Well, Billy, what do you think Heaven is going to be like?"

Well, there are some things we know. But, there are mysteries known only to God. There is a mystery to Hell; there is a mystery to Heaven. I personally believe that the Bible teaches that Heaven is a literal place. You say, "Do you think it is one of the stars or do you think it is one of the plants, or where do you think it is?"

I don't know. The Bible doesn't tell us. I can't even speculate. I do know that the scientists tell us there are a hundred billion stars in our galaxy. Now we don't measure distance in miles. We measure it in light years. With light traveling at the rate of 186,000 miles a second, eleven million miles to the minute, the sun is only eight light minutes from us. One light year is six trillion miles. Our galaxy, just our galaxy, is one hundred thousand light years in diameter. There are one thousand million galaxies, and in each galaxy it is estimated there are one hundred thousand million stars and planets. I believe that out there somewhere God can find some place to put us in Heaven. I'm not worried where it is going to be. I know it is going to be where Jesus is.

Jesus said, "I go to prepare a place for you." And I read in the Bible that Abraham looked for a city whose builder and maker was God, and I know that the Scripture says that "Here we have no continuing city." There is nothing permanent in this life. There is only one permanent thing in life, and that is impermanence. Nothing lasts. Every day you read the obituary column in *The New York Times* or one of the other newspapers. They died and left it all. One fellow left in his will—he was a Texas millionaire—that he wanted to be buried in a gold Cadillac. And as he was going down in the grave in his gold Cadillac, one of the grave diggers said, "Boy, that's really living."

Not only is Heaven a place, but the Bible teaches that Heaven is going to be Home. The Bible says that those of us who know Christ—the moment you accept Christ, you become a citizen of Heaven. Now we are citizens of two worlds. I am a citizen of this earth, but I'm a citizen of another world. I am a citizen of Heaven because of what Christ did on the Cross. And in this world with its secularism and its materialism and all of its hostile forces I'm living for God, I'm a stranger and a pilgrim. The Bible refers to that in several places. We are strangers and we are pilgrims. "They were strangers and pilgrims on the earth," says Hebrews 11. 1 Peter 2 says, "I beseech you as strangers and pilgrims." Our citizenship is in Heaven. Now as good citizens of this earth we ought to vote. As good citizens we ought to be interested in our community. As good citizens we ought to help every good project in our community. As good citizens we ought to be interested in all the social problems that we face. As good citizens we ought to do what we can to make this a better place in which to live. But we are citizens of two worlds . . . this world and the future world. We are citizens of Heaven. My citizenship is there. Now I've already lived most of my life here. I am fifty years old. I'm not likely to live to be a hundred. In fact, I will be very happy if I make it to sixty or sixty-five. I'll be happy if I just make it through this service.

We never know. Most of my life, though, by the law of averages, is gone. I'm on the sunset side now. I'm already a grandfather and very proud of it. And I'm glad that I'm a citizen of the future world. Now you think of all the emphasis we put on retirement centers and senior citizens, and all the benefits of retirement. You'd have an idea, wouldn't you, by reading the ads and hearing all the propaganda that, the moment you retire you are in Heaven. Well, I go to a lot of these places and I know a lot of older people, and the first year that they are retired, they are full of energy. But then after a while they begin to settle down and they begin to realize that the next step is the casket. And the aches and the pains and the problems of old age—it is not quite what the ad said it would be unless Christ is in your heart. Because you see, you experience Heaven the moment you receive Christ. Heaven comes to live in your heart, because Christ is heaven. He said, "The kingdom of Heaven is within you."

And you know in the future life those of us who know

Christ are going to be like Jesus. How would you like live in a whole world where everybody was like Jesu Well, that's what it says . . .

"Beloved, now are we the sons of God, and it doth n yet appear what we shall be: but we know that, when shall appear, we shall be like him; for we shall see him he is" (1 John 3:2).

Now in Heaven there is not going to be any racial di crimination. There is not going to be any poverty. The is not going to be any war. The policemen won't hav anything to do. Oh, what a glorious world it is going to b —Heaven! Everything that that word means, everythin that you ever dreamed of—the Utopia that we dreame of and thought that maybe we could build on this earth and have failed, is going to be in Heaven.

And then Heaven is going to be a place of service Now you're not just going to go there and sit under palm tree and have a pretty girl waving a palm branc over you. Lots of people have the idea that that is wha Heaven is like. One of the great religions of the worl teaches that. It says, "You're going to have a thousand girls to wait on you." No, that's not what the Bible says It says we are going to work. I imagine that is going to b hard on some. But we are going to work, because it say in Revelation 22:3, "His servants shall serve him."

You know I've got the feeling that we are going to b able to travel from planet to planet, and the thing that science is now beginning to catch a glimpse of we are going to see completely and fully. And all of these scientific things are going to be an actuality in Heaven. And do you know how fast I think we are going to travel? This is my own private speculation. This is not in the Bible. Don't go out of here and quote it. You know the fastest way to travel somewhere? Thought. Think it. All right, I think I am on Mars. I am there. What is that program on television where the witch twitches her nose, and instantly she is in another place? She thinks it. Well, this is a little glimpse of what it may be like. We can think our way through the universe, serving God as ambassadors to other planets, because we are going to be the Sons of

HEAVEN AND HELL

God. We are going to be something that people on other planets probably never dreamed they would be. We are going to be the actual Sons of the living God who runs this whole universe. Now that's incredible. It's almost impossible to believe, but this is what the Bible teaches. We are the Sons of God.

And Heaven is going to be a place where all mysteries are going to be cleared up. Why did we have a certain amount of suffering down here? Why were loved ones taken at a particular moment when they were? We are going to understand something of the enormity of sin. We are going to understand the problem of evil. We are going to understand what the devil was all about, and why God allowed him to exist as long as he did. We'll know something of the price that Christ paid on the Cross that we cannot know now. When He said, "My God, My God, why hast Thou forsaken me?"—none of us can understand what went on at that moment, but on that Day, we will understand.

We will know why there is a Hell. We will understand why God moves in a mysterious way His wonders to perform. You know there are ten thousand questions I want to ask the Lord as soon as I get there. I want to ask Him some of these questions that these college kids have asked me that I couldn't answer, because they are just mysteries in the Bible that we don't know all the answers to. We must take them by faith.

Now I have staked personally, and many of you have, my eternal future on the fact that this Bible is true and Jesus knew what He was talking about. I can't make you do it. I ask you to do it—that's a commitment that you as an individual have a right to reject. You can reject it. You don't have to believe it. That's your privilege; that's your freedom of choice. I myself also have the same freedom, and I accepted it, and it answers many questions in my life and gives me a peace, a security, and a serenity.

You say, "Billy, you're dreaming."

Someone wrote a hymn. I think it was Gypsy Smith. He said, "If I am dreaming, let me dream on, my sins are gone." It is a wonderful dream.

And you know Heaven is going to be the place of the final coronation of the King of Kings. What a day that is going to be! The Bible says, "There will be written on Him, King of Kings, and Lord of Lords." You and I are going to be present at the coronation of Jesus Christ when He is crowned King of the Universe. I am looking forward to that day. My seat is reserved. It was bought not with my silver and gold. It was bought with the blood of Christ on the Cross. What a time that is going to be!

You know when Handel—George Frederick Handel—wrote *The Messiah* he was in poor health and poor financial condition. His right arm and his right side were almost useless by paralysis, and all of a sudden the "Hallelujah Chorus" came to him. When it was first sung in 1743, I believe it was at Covent Garden in London. When they came to that chorus—"The Lord Omnipotent reigneth, King of Kings and Lord of Lords," the King of Great Britain, the most powerful country in the world at that time, rose to his feet and so did that vast audience,—to acknowledge the "King of Kings and Lord of Lords."

Listen, we Christians don't have to go around with our shoulders bent and discouraged and despondent. We are on our way to Heaven. This is not our home, and this is not our world. We are going to help all we can, but we are on our way to a better world.

And you know when you get that perspective, you can be a better servant of the Lord right here. And you know the Bible, by warnings and threats and invitations and commands, urges people to make that decision. Make that decision now and receive Christ as your Lord and your Savior.

You know *The Times* told this morning about Neil Armstrong who is scheduled to plant his foot on the moon at 2:17 a.m., Eastern Daylight Time, on July 21. And in yesterday's paper we saw pictures of Neil Armstrong practicing the landing of his craft so that he would be ready.

Now, if you intend to set your feet in Heaven, you are going to have to do a little practicing down here. You've got to rehearse by planting your feet on the Rock of Ages, Jesus Christ.

Do you know Him as your Savior? Is your sin forgiven?

We had an election here as we have already heard, and I remember a story that when Mayor La Guardia was mayor of this city or when he was a judge, I guess, a man was brought before him during the depression. He had stolen a loaf of bread to feed his family. And the mayor had to fine him $50. Then the mayor looked at the audience in the courtroom and said, "This court is not only one of justice, it is one of mercy." And then he fined everyone in the courtroom $1 for allowing conditions to exist where a man had to steal to provide for his family. And he gave the money to the man and said, "Pay your fine and go your way and sin no more," and that is exactly what Jesus did. He paid the fine for us. He took the hell and the judgment and the destruction and the end of that broad road for us. Now God says, "I love you. I forgive you. Go and sin no more."

You start through that narrow gate and live on the narrow road, and you are going to be in Heaven.

Which road are you on tonight? Which direction are you traveling? Are you going toward destruction or are you going toward Life? Which way? You can make the choice tonight. You can take the first step. Now it's costly. It's not easy to go through that narrow gate, and it's not easy to follow Christ. But it is a glorious and wonderful experience even here on this earth—the joy, the peace, the security, the sense of forgiveness, that He gives you—all this and Heaven, too—by a choice that you make.

You say, "Well, why did God make it so simple? He made it simple so everybody could enter—the blind man, the poor man, the deaf man—the black, the white, the yellow, the red—anybody can believe. Anybody can receive. Anybody can come by faith." He said, "Whosoever will, let him come." The offer is open to everyone here tonight. Will you come?

Delivered June 17, 1969

VI.

TRUTH AND FREEDOM

I'm going to ask that we bow our heads in prayer. Every head bowed and every eye closed. There are many of you here tonight and many watching by television who have a need in your life. You're not quite sure what it is. You've tried to find satisfaction and fulfillment and peace and happiness in a thousand different ways, but you've failed. Tonight you can make the great commitment that can change and transform your entire life. You could commit your life to Christ. And that little simple act of commitment can change the direction you're now going and bring about a whole new situation in your life. You can put your trust and your faith and your confidence in Christ tonight.

Our Father and our God, we thank Thee and praise Thee that at this moment of history we have a Gospel of forgiveness and peace and hope, that we do not despair as other men. We as Christians are not pessimistic. We're optimistic because Christ has been raised from the dead, and we know that righteousness is going to triumph ultimately because of Him. We pray tonight that many in this Garden and those watching by television will be convinced of their need of the Savior and be drawn to Him. For we ask it in His Name. Amen.

Now, every night we have many distinguished people I would like to introduce, both on the platform and in the audience. We have a lot of people from show business. We have many people who are leaders of industry, leaders of labor, civil rights leaders. Many of them are distinguished in their own fields. We have many religious leaders who sit on the platform and out in the audience night

TRUTH AND FREEDOM

after night. And I was just thinking how many men on the platform tonight have been chairmen of former Crusades.

I could go down the list of people who are here tonight and night after night. We welcome you. I wish we had time for each one of you to come and preach a sermon and tell us what is in your heart because there are many here who could do just that.

Tonight I want to turn to John's Gospel, the 8th chapter, the 32nd verse: "And ye shall know the truth, and the truth shall make you free."

These are the words of our Lord Jesus Christ. He's having a debate with some of the religious leaders of His day, and He said, "Ye shall know the truth." Now that word "shall" could be translated "must." You must know the truth if you're to be free. Tonight I want to talk about truth and freedom. We hear a great deal about those today.

Some years ago I heard about a clergyman who had a friend who was an actor; and the actor was drawing large crowds of people, and the clergyman was preaching to few in the church. And so he said to his actor friend, "Why is it that you draw great crowds and I have no audience at all? Your words are sheer fiction, and mine are unchangeable truth." And the actor's answer was quite simple. "I present my fiction as though it were truth; you present your truth as though it were fiction." And I fear that so often we Christians give the idea that the truth is fiction by the way we live and by the lack of dedication to the teachings of our Lord.

You know there's an old Scottish oath upon which our American oath is based, and it reads this way, "I pledge before Almighty God, before whom I will give an answer on the day of judgment to tell the truth, the whole truth, and nothing but the truth." Jesus said, "Ye shall know the truth, and the truth shall make you free."

The universities until a few years ago were places where people spent their time searching for truth. At least we thought that. The university was a place for research; it was a place for study; it was a place for dialogue and exchange of ideas, a place of learning. But now we've seen a revolution take place on the campuses of American universities during the past few months. Many faculty members are being intimidated. A faculty member was quoted in the press from a New York university, "We can no longer teach the truth as we see it on our campus because we are threatened with violence."

And so academic freedom in America is in jeopardy, in very serious jeopardy, as many universities are becoming centers for political action.

And yet another strange thing is taking place, which Bill Bright was telling me a few minutes ago. There has never been such an open door to the Gospel on campus as there is today. Students are listening to many voices, but at least one of the voices students are listening to is the voice of the Bible and the voice of the Gospel of Christ. Jesus said, "Ye shall know the truth, and the truth shall make you free."

Now in this passage of Scripture, Jesus discussed two personalities. He discussed God on the one hand, who is truth, and Satan on the other, who is a liar and the author of lies. Now here's what Jesus said. He was pretty rough in some of the things He said. He turned to these religious leaders and said, "You are of your father the devil, and the lusts of your father you will do: he was a murderer from the beginning and abode not in the truth, because there is no truth in him. When he speaketh a lie, he speaketh of his own: for he is a liar, and the father of lies." Jesus said that there is the lie and there is the truth. And in 2 Thessalonians, the second chapter, we are told that in the latter days of this age there will be a system called "The Lie." "They shalt be sent strong delusion, that they should believe a lie." A great delusion will sweep over the people of that generation. They will believe a lie, and they will reject the truth. Many people think we're living in that generation.

The Apostle Paul said in the first chapter of Romans that the people of that day had changed the truth of God into a lie. Now we in America are in danger of rejecting the truth of this Book. We are rejecting the Ten Commandments and the Sermon on the Mount as the basis for morality. We are changing it for a lie. We are saying that it's all right if it's a meaningful experience. That was what we said two years ago. Now it's all right under any conditions, many of our people are saying. You can come now to various cities of America and see that the moral dam has broken in the theater, in literature, in motion pictures. We've exchanged the truth of God for a lie, and the end is going to be judgment unless we quickly change back.

That's why a crusade like this is so important. It's important that we Americans realize that the security of the nation is involved in morality and spirituality. And I don't think we can have a moral awakening in the country or a moral reversal without a spiritual awakening. God will have to send it in answer to prayer.

And then, secondly, not only do we exchange the truth of God for a lie, but Paul said in Romans, the first chapter and the 18th verse, "Who hold the truth in unrighteousness." In other words, you can know the truth and not live it. This is holding the truth of God in unrighteousness. The Bible says the wrath of God is against such people, and that's why Christ was so bitter in His denunciation of the hypocrites. You hold the truth intellectually, but you don't live it. God said, "You serve me with your lips but your heart is far from me."

You see, we have our name on a church roll. Most Americans do. Eighty percent of all adult Americans are identified with a church or synagogue, but we don't live it. I was in a prison some time ago; and the governor of the state, trying to please me, said, "Billy, you'll be interested to know that 65 percent of our convicts are Baptist." Well, I laughed as you did, and then I began to think about it. What a sad commentary on the church! It's easy to get into the church. We have neglected discipline in the church; we've neglected discipleship. I want to talk about that tomorrow night. What kind of a commitment do we have to make to be a real Christian in 1969? You can hold the truth in unrighteousness, and that brings about the wrath of God.

And then, thirdly, Paul said, ". . . judgment according to truth . . . ," Romans 2:2, "but we are sure that the judgment of God is according to truth . . ." In other words, some day God is going to judge the world. Yes, there's a day of judgment coming. Just as certain as I'm standing here, a day of judgment is coming and God is going to judge us according to "The Truth." Did we live by "The Truth"? Did we believe "The Truth"? Did we accept "The Truth"? What was our attitude toward "The Truth"? Did we change The Truth for a lie, or did we hold The Truth in unrighteousness? God will hold us accountable, the Scripture says.

Jesus said, "You must know the truth, and the truth will make you free."

Now, you know, that's what philosophy has been doing, that's what science does, and that's what we do in psychology. In every field of study and in every discipline we're searching for truth. We're trying to find what the laws are. We're trying to find what the truth is. Now early in childhood we learned the truth that fire is hot. We learned that ice is cold. We learned that doing wrong makes us feel guilty and doing good makes us feel good. We learned that early. Jesus said, "You must know the truth."

But what is the truth? That was the question of Pilate. He said, "What is truth?" Schleiermacher, the great philosopher in Germany, was sitting in a park late at night when a policeman approached him and asked, "Who are you?" And the great philosopher said, "That's a big question. I wish I knew."

Sir Isaac Newton, the great scientist, one time wrote before his death, he said, "My life seems to have been only like a little boy playing on the seashore and diverting myself now and then in finding a smoother pebble or a prettier shell, while the great ocean of truth lay all undiscovered before me."

You see, all of us are really on a quest for truth. What is the truth about myself? Where did I come from? Why in the world did God ever put us on this planet, if there is a God? Some ask. And where are we going? Is there a life after death? I'm searching for answers. All of us are, consciously or unconsciously. We ask ourselves these questions. "What is truth?" The same question Pilate asked two thousand years ago.

And that's why a lot of these kids are taking LSD and mind-expansion psychedelic drugs. They're trying to find some experiences that will lead them into some sort of a spiritual truth. Now truth is important in mathematics; it's important in chemistry; it's important in science; and it's important in the spiritual life. It's important in morality. It's important to find the truth. Jesus said, "You shall know the truth." No guesswork, no speculation, is allowed. In aviation you can make one mistake and you may crash into another plane. You must know the truth and act on the truth.

Now Job said, "I know my Redeemer lives." The Apostle Paul said, "I know in whom I have believed." The Apostle John said, "You can know that you're saved." The Bible teaches that you can know the truth. You can find the truth. You can believe the truth. But what is the truth?

Now many times when you find out the truth about yourself, you don't like it. Truth is not always pleasant. I knew a man a few years ago who was feeling in perfect health and he went for a routine examination. The doctor found that he had cancer, a very serious type of malignancy in his lung. He was bitter at the doctor for telling him the truth. He said, "Doctor, I've always been afraid that I would have cancer, but I wish you hadn't told me." "Ye shall know the truth."

What is the truth? Notice, Jesus said, "*the* truth." He didn't say "a truth." Just not any kind of truth, "The Truth." Every religion and every philosophy may have some of the truth, but there is only one place you can find all the truth. Where is it? Jesus said, "Everyone that is of the truth heareth my voice." Buddha said, "I'm still searching for truth" at the end of his life. But Jesus made this astounding claim. Jesus said, "I am the truth." Jesus said, "I am the embodiment of all truths," and if you're going to get to heaven you've got to believe that. And you've got to commit your life to it.

Well, you say that anybody who would come along and

say, "I am the embodiment of all truth," must be mentally deranged. He's an egomaniac. Yes, you can make a case for that. Or, maybe Jesus just told a lie. He knew it wasn't true, and He just lied. Yes, that's one of the options. But suppose He *is* the truth. Suppose He is the embodiment of all truth and you rejected and exchanged the truth for a lie. Then you have made a fatal error for eternity.

Now I personally believe that Jesus is the truth. I believe that He is the embodiment of all truth. I have accepted that by faith; and when I took that step and took that stand, it changed my life.

Listen to that passage Dr. Dan Potter read a moment ago. Listen to it again. "He is the image of the invisible God, the firstborn of every creature: for by Him"—listen to this—"for by Him were all things created that are in heaven, and that are on the earth, visible and invisible, whether they be thrones, or dominions, or principalities, or powers: all things were created by Him, and for Him: and He is before all things, and by Him all things hold together." All this gigantic universe with its billions of stars and planets was created by Him, for Him, and it holds together and operates by certain laws because of Him. We know the atom and the molecules, but we don't know what keeps it all together. This desk, science tells us, is a mass of swirling molecules. Science doesn't know the answer to that yet. When they finally find the answer to what holds this whole thing together, they're going to come up with Jesus, according to the Bible.

You say, "Billy, do you believe *that* in this scientific age? You mean you . . ." Yes, I believe it. I've accepted that as the Word of the living God, and when I accepted that and it dawned on me that everything that Buddha was looking for and everything that Mohammed was looking for and everything that all the great philosophers of history have been looking for—the ultimate final complete answer, is Jesus Christ, the Son of the living God. And it's very simple. And He made it so simple that you can know the truth. A blind man, a deaf man, a black man, a white man, a yellow man, a red man, can come and know the truth. The educated man can know the truth; the uneducated can know the truth. I know people who don't have any education at all, and they know this truth and it gives them a satisfaction and a joy. And I know professors at the great universities, and I know some of the great scientists. They have come and accepted this as the truth and bowed in humility before the Christ back of science, and it's changed their lives.

You remember the great Swiss theologian, Dr. Karl Barth. He was in this country a few years ago; he died last year. And Dr. Barth was probably in his generation the greatest theologian in the world, and a great philosopher as well. I did not always agree with him, but he was my friend and I respected him. And while he was in this country, a student of one of the seminaries said, "Dr. Barth, what is the greatest truth that ever crossed your mind?" All the seminary students were sitting on the edge of their seats to hear some great, profound, deep, complicated answer. And Dr. Barth raised his great shaggy gray head slowly and looked at the student and said, "Jesus loves me, this I know, for the Bible tells me so."

Truth! The profoundest truth in simplicity so that anybody can come, and anybody can believe, even children. Whittier once said, "We search the world for truth. We call the good and the pure and the beautiful from graven stone and written scroll, from all the plowed fields of the soul, and weary seekers of the best, we come back laden from the crest, to find that all the stage is set in the Book our mothers read." It's here in the Bible.

Jesus Christ, the story of Christ. Here's the truth, and Jesus said this in that same chapter, the 24th verse. He said, "If ye believe not . . ." Listen to this. "If ye believe not that I am he, you will die in your sins." "If you believe not that I am the embodiment of all truth, you're going to die in your sins." You must come and believe and accept and commit.

Yes, Christ claimed to be ultimate truth, and Jesus told the truth. He told the truth about sin. Where does the lust, the greed, the pride, the hate, the jealousy, and the fighting come from? Why do people hate each other?

Why do they fight and kill and every generation has a war? The Bible tells us man has a disease of the heart called "Sin." For from within, out of the hearts of men, proceed evil thoughts and adulteries and fornications and murders and thefts and covetousness and wickedness and deceit and blasphemy and pride. All of these things come from within and defile a man."

We're suffering from only one disease in the world. Our basic problem is not a race problem. Our basic problem is not a poverty problem. Our basic problem is not a war problem. Our basic problem is a heart problem. We need to get the heart changed, the heart transformed. That's why Jesus said you must be born again. You must have a new nature, a new heart, that will be dominated by love.

Ah, but we go out and say we ought to love each other, but we soon find that we don't have the capacity to love each other. Where are we going to get it? We get it from Jesus. You see, the Spirit of God comes into our hearts the moment we receive Christ, and He begins to produce in our hearts love, joy, peace, patience and self-control. All of these fruits of the Spirit are produced supernaturally by the Holy Spirit when you receive Christ. He told the truth about what is wrong with the world.

And then He told the truth about our social responsibilities, our responsibility to our fellow man; in the 25th chapter of Matthew, beginning at verse 35, you'll find it. People were hungry, they were sick, they were tired, they were cold, and they were in prison. They were visited and they were helped. And at the judgment Jesus commended them. They said, "But Lord, we didn't know that we visited you. We didn't know that we fed you. We didn't know that we did that for you." Jesus said, "If you did it unto the least of these, you've done it unto me." And every time that you give of your time and your energy and your money to help those in need, you're helping Jesus, you're giving to Him.

And then He told the truth about judgment. He warned us to flee the wrath of God. "Every idle word that men shall speak they will give an account in the day of judgment," He said. There is a judgment coming.

He told the truth about repentance. He said, "Except you repent you shall perish." You say, "But how do I repent?" You say, "O God, I've sinned. I'm willing to change my way of living. I'm willing to live in a new dimension of life. I'm willing to follow you and serve you, no matter what the cost." That's repentance. And Jesus said if you don't repent you're going to perish. He told the truth about that.

He told the truth about conversion. He said, "Except ye be converted and become as little children you cannot enter the kingdom of heaven." Be converted. We're frightened of that word in the modern church. We use it in everything else but not in the church.

Young people want an "experience." They want something that means something. They have their "happenings," they want to do their "thing," they want to take their drug; and they want their "kicks." But in the church we've stifled out any kind of religious experience. Jesus said you need to be converted. I can remember the day I was converted. I had an experience with God. It wasn't an emotional experience with me. With some people it is. There is nothing wrong with emotion. We've certainly got emotional intellectualism today on campus. I see these intellectuals on campus on television and they're shouting it up pretty loud for their cause and what they believe. Now we allow emotion for everything except Christ. If anybody sheds a tear about religion, they say, "Too much emotion." That's one of the devil's lies and the devil's tricks so that we've lost all feeling and joy in our faith, and all the excitement and the thrill that these early Christians had are gone.

Jesus said you need to be converted. Now the word "conversion" simply means to change, turn around. You're going in one direction on the broad road that leads to destruction. Turn around and go in the right direction, go the narrow road that leads to eternal life. That's what it means. Conversion, to change, to turn around.

Has that happened to you? Have you changed your way of living? Have you had an experience with Christ?

Do you know Him personally? "Ye shall know the truth, and the truth shall make you free."

Now I know that there are many people who think they're free already, and they don't know Christ. They think they know how to live. The Bible says there is a way, there's a way outside of Christ, that seems right unto man. It seems the right thing, but the end is death and judgment. I have a little boy; and when he was much smaller, three years of age, we borrowed a boat down in Florida, and we were going down the river. My friend, Lee Fisher, was in the stern trying to get the fishing gear ready, and I was running the boat. And my little boy, Ned, said, "Daddy, I want to run this boat." And I said, "No, I don't think you know how to run it." "Oh, yes, I know exactly how to do it," he said. He pushed my hands out of the way, so I let him have the wheel; and he headed right toward the rocks. You see, we all say, "Lord, we know how to run our lives; don't you interfere. We're going to be all right. There is nothing we can't handle." But Jesus warns you that you're heading for the rocks. You're in trouble. Emptiness, neurosis, complexes of various sorts, set in and ultimately, the judgment.

Repent, be converted, while you can. "Now is the accepted time. Today is the day of salvation."

Now what does the truth do? It sets you free. "Ye shall know the truth, and the truth shall set you free." From what? First, Christ's truth sets you free, from the penalty of sin. Yes, there's a penalty to sin. Now we're all sinners; every one of us is a sinner, and we're all under the penalty of sin which is death. "The wages of sin is death," the Bible says.

Death carries with it the idea of separation from God in this life and in the life to come. The rich young ruler came to Jesus and said, "What must I do to inherit eternal life?" He wanted life here and now, but he also wanted life to come. He felt the deadness of his spirit and the deadness of his soul, but he wasn't willing to pay the price. There's a price if you come to Christ. The rich young ruler tried to bargain with Jesus. He wanted Jesus to lower the price. He wanted Jesus to change the rules for him so that he could get into the kingdom; but Jesus will never lower the cost; He'll never compromise. He'll never change the rules.

You've got to come to Christ just as people did two thousand years ago if you're ever to get to heaven. We live in sophisticated America. We thought we had all the answers, but look at us. Sending a man to the moon with one hand and building gigantic bombs and rockets with the other to blow the world to pieces! Campuses torn apart, society being ripped apart! No, we don't have all the answers, because, you see, we rejected the truth. We rejected Christ.

Receive Christ in your life. Let Him come and put the pieces back together in your life. He will forgive your sin, and give you purpose and meaning in your life, and take the penalty of sin away. "There's therefore then no judgment to them that are in Christ." He removes the penalty.

Secondly, He can set you free from the power of sin. He said, "Whosoever committeth sin is the servant of sin." But when you receive Christ, this power of sin to dominate your life is broken. "Sin shall no longer dominate in your life," said Paul to the Romans. "Sin shall no longer have dominion over you." You can reckon yourself to be dead to sin. So that although sin may be in your life—it doesn't dominate you. You don't make sin a practice in your life. You have power over sin. The Spirit of God living in you through a new nature God gives you.

And then, thirdly, He sets us free ultimately from the very presence of sin. You read the Revelation, the 21st chapter and the 22nd chapter, and you will see the most glorious description of heaven and the future world. On the outside of this new world is a Utopia that is called Heaven. God is building it for those who trust Him. The Scripture says without are the sorcerers, the warmongers, the murderers, the idolaters, and whosoever loveth and maketh a lie. All liars, all people that live a lie will be on the outside, he said, would be excluded and banished from the presence of God. Jesus said, "I am the truth. Ye shall know the truth and the truth shall set you free."

There was an ad in *The New York Times* today, a

whole page, that said, "Come to Life." Great big boxcar letters. "Come to Life."

I'm asking you tonight to come to life, come to the truth, to the source of life, to Jesus Christ, the Son of God. Someday we'll be removed from the very presence of sin and the devil and all lies. We shall overcome, some day. 'Till then we can have God's life right here on this earth. We can have a little bit of heaven, we can be set free from the bondage of sin and slavery and the devil right now. Christ can set you free. I'm asking you tonight by faith to receive Him, to receive the truth.

Notice I said "by faith." You cannot come with your mind alone because your mind was affected by sin. You have to come as a little child. "Except ye become as children and be converted," said Jesus. You have to come like a little child by simple, child-like faith and receive Him. And if you will He comes into your heart, gives you a new nature, and you can go out and live a new life.

Now it's hard and it's tough and it's rough to follow Christ. I don't want you to come under any false illusions, but when you make that commitment, you don't go back into the world and back to your house and back to your neighborhood to live the Christian life alone. He goes with you.

I'm going to ask you to come tonight and receive Him openly and publicly.

Delivered June 18, 1969

VII.

LET'S BE RADICAL

I want you to turn with me to the 14th chapter of Luke's Gospel, beginning with verse 25:

"And there went great multitudes with him: and he turned, and said unto them, If any man come to me, and hate not his father, and mother, and wife, and children, and brethren, and sisters, yea, and his own life also, he cannot be my disciple. And whosoever doth not bear his cross, and come after me, cannot be my disciple. For which of you, intending to build a tower, sitteth not down first, and counteth the cost, whether he have sufficient to finish it?"

Then turn with me to Matthew's Gospel, the 16th chapter, verse 24. These words:

"Then said Jesus unto his disciples, if any man will come after me, let him deny himself, and take up his cross, and follow me."

Three things Jesus said: let a man deny himself, let him take up his Cross, and let him follow Me.

In a book called *The Age of Longing* an American girl married a radical revolutionary in Paris. She had lost her faith at an American university—lost all the religious faith she had and all the things her parents had told her and had gone to Paris and there she met a revolutionary—a radical. She was asked why she married him. She said, "He's the first person I have ever known who believes something strong enough to die for it. And although I don't believe exactly as he does, I was attracted to this man who had found a cause."

I find that young people today are looking for a cause and they are not looking for something easy.

A university student in Moscow told one of my colleagues some time ago when he was visiting there, "You Christians say that you are going to win the world, but we've done more in fifty years than you've done in two thousand years. And do you know why? It is because you are uncommitted. We are. We will win, you see."

I have a letter which a radical young person, a radical student, wrote to his girlfriend. Would you like to hear it? Here is what he said:

"We radicals have a high casualty rate. We are the ones who get shot and hung and tarred and feathered and jailed and slandered and ridiculed and fired from our jobs and every other way made as uncomfortable as possible. A certain percentage of us get killed. We radicals don't have the time for movies or concerts. We've been described as fanatics. We are. Our lives are dominated by one great overshadowing factor, the struggle for revolution. We radicals have a philosophy of life which no amount of money can buy. We have a cause to fight for, a definite purpose in life, and we subordinate our petty personal selves into a great movement of humanity. And if our personal lives seem hard or our egos appear to suffer through subordination to the cause, then we are adequately compensated by the thought that each of us in his small way is helping to do something to make a better world. There is one thing about which I am in dead earnest and that is the radical cause. It is my life, my business, my religion, my hobby, my sweetheart, my wife, my mystery, my bread, and my meat. I work at it in the daytime and I dream of it at night. Its hold on me grows, not lessens, as time goes on. Therefore (to his girlfriend), I cannot carry on a friendship, a love affair, or even a conversation without relating to this force which both drives and guides my life. I evaluate people, books, ideas, actions, according to how they effect radical causes and by their attitudes toward it. I have already been in jail because of my ideas, and if necessary I am ready to go before a firing squad."

I am using these illustrations for a purpose. This sounds very much like the writings of the early church.

This was the kind of dedication to Christ a group of revolutionary young people had two thousand years ago when they went out to change the world with love instead of with hate—young men who had committed their lives to a Person called Jesus whom they believed had been raised from the dead, and they were ready to die for His cause.

Somewhere along the line we have lost the meaning of discipleship. We've lost the meaning of what it really means to follow Jesus Christ. And I think what we see going on in the college campuses today is beginning to teach us something about dedication and what small minorities can do if they are dedicated to a cause.

And when you come to the Bible, to the Old and the New Testaments, God does not demand any less of us in our relationship to Jesus Christ. You look in the Old Testament and see what God demanded of Abraham. God said one day, "Abraham, I want you to go out to Mount Moriah and I want you to take your little son, the son you have waited so many years for, the son whom you love more than anything in the world, and I want you to offer him on the altar."

Abraham obeyed God and went out and put his son on an altar and took a long gleaming knife and was plunging it toward his son's heart in obedience to God when God stopped him in mid-air. He said, "That's far enough, Abraham. I know now that you are ready to go all the way with Me."

Or take Moses. Moses was the foster son of Pharaoh's daughter. He was possibly the heir to the throne of Egypt. He could have possibly been the Emperor of the greatest empire in the world of his day. He had all the riches and all the glory and all the power that a man could have, but he deliberately turned his back on it in order to suffer with the people of God. God demanded that Moses give up everything in order to be used, and then God set him on the back side of the desert to study, to pray, and to grow and to learn.

Or Joseph. Joseph was sold by his brethren—had to go down to Egypt a stranger. He could have compromised.

Nobody would have ever known it, except God. And Potiphar's wife was very beautiful, alluring and very sexy. She tried to get him to sleep with her. Joseph was a young teenager hundreds of miles from home. Nobody would have ever known. He knew that he could have advanced in the kingdom by having the favor of Potiphar's wife, but he refused. He left his cloak behind when she grabbed at him and it meant prison for him and he was sentenced to death. God was testing to see if this young man really meant it.

Or there is Daniel. They said, "Daniel, no more prayer in Babylon. If you do, you are going to the lions' den."

Daniel prayed three times a day and believed in God and trusted in God. Even though he was the prime minister of the country, they put him in a lions' den, and Daniel did not know that God was going to close the lions' mouths. God was calling upon him to pay the supreme price, and he was willing to do it.

The Apostle Paul in the New Testament who carried the message of Christ in that early church said in 2 Corinthians 11, "Five times I received forty stripes, save one. Three times I was beaten with a rod. Once I was stoned and three times I suffered shipwreck. A night and a day I have been in the deep; In journeyings often, in perils of waters, in perils of robbers, in perils by mine own countrymen, in perils by the heathen, in perils in the city, in perils in the wilderness, in perils in the sea, in perils among false brethren; In weariness and painfulness, in watchings often, in hunger and thirst, in cold and nakedness. I carried this message of the Gospel." That is what it cost.

And Jesus is saying to us in 1969, "Take up your Cross, deny self, follow Me, and we can change the world," and He set the pace. You see we seek riches, but He was rich and yet He became poor for our sakes that we might become rich. We seek comfort, but the "foxes have holes and the birds have nests and the Son of God has nowhere to lay His head." We seek acceptance, but He was despised and rejected of men. We want to avoid suffering, but He was wounded for our transgressions. He was bruised for our iniquities. We are self-centered, but He said, "I lay down my life for others." He was centered in other people. Christ taught it, He lived it, He demands it of us, no less.

Then said Jesus to His disciples, "If any man, would come after Me, let him deny self and take up the cross and follow Me."

Are you willing to do that tonight in 1959 if it means everything? He lays down the condition, and only a few in our generation are willing to pay that kind of a price.

You see when you pick up the New Testament the words you read about Christianity are verbs, not nouns. The words "fight," "suffer," "work"—those are the verbs that moved the early church to discipleship—a discipline under the Lordship of Christ.

And a Christian is described in the New Testament as a soldier who must suffer hardship. "Now therefore endure suffering and hardness as a good soldier of Jesus Christ," Paul wrote to Timothy. He asks you to enlist in His army. He'll send you to boot camp, maybe to a Bible school or maybe to a Christian school, or maybe He'll send you in a different direction to learn and to study. God uses only prepared men. It will be tough and it will be rough.

And then the Bible says that we are like boxers. Now they are going to have a championship fight in Madison Square Garden on Monday night.

And we are described in the Bible as boxers, who practice self-restraint, and discipline. We are like an athlete.

Jesus said, "Come unto Me and learn of Me. Be disciplined." The word "disciple" means "learner"—"a disciplined learner."

"If any man will come after me." Notice you have a personal choice to make. You can't come after Him until you come to Him, and many of you have never really come to Him. You have never received Him as your Lord and your Savior. There is no cause that really dominates your life. The vast majority of young people in this country are uncommitted—uncommitted to anything. And the ones that do get committed to something—we hear about.

But the vast majority of American young people are not committed. I am asking you to be committed to the greatest cause of all, the cause of Christ.

And if millions of young people can march in China for Mao Tse-tung, we ought to be able to march for Christ. And if they are willing to memorize the writings and the sayings of Mao in that little red book, we ought to be willing to study the Bible and memorize passages so that it becomes a sword in our hands.

"Let us deny ourselves," He says. How do you deny yourself? What does that mean? Does that mean deny yourself a milkshake, deny yourself a Coca-Cola, deny yourself a drug, deny yourself alcohol and sex? What does it mean? It means that you deny self. It is the opposite of selfishness. It means that love is to dominate your life. Love for God? "Thou shalt love the Lord thy God with all thy heart, mind and soul and love for your fellowmen." You deny self. You put God first, you put others second, and you put yourself last.

But it means something even deeper. It means the denial of all the temptations that come to young people today. Nobody can follow Christ and commit sex outside of marriage. It means denying yourself even in the realm of food. You become temperate about food and drink because the Bible has a lot to say about gluttony. It means that you deny yourself sinful pleasures . . . pleasures that are wrong. You know they are wrong. It means to deny yourself pride—intellectual and religious pride, which is wrong. There is a certain type of pride of accomplishment that is right. There is a certain amount of ambition that is right, but if the ambition is to build you up and glorify you, then it is wrong. This text means to deny this desire to be somebody on your own, to be recognized and admired. It means that you cannot pass your neighbor by who has a need, like Dives, the rich man, who passed Lazarus by. Now his sin wasn't throwing rocks at Lazarus; he didn't kick him as he went by; he just ignored him.

It means that you become a nonconformist. Now you see most young people today are dressing alike, looking alike, acting alike, and reading the same books and you are afraid to be different. If the fellows go around without any socks, you want to go around without socks. You want to dress alike, look alike, be alike so you won't be looked on as different, or as a square. But the Bible is calling you to be something else—to come out from among all the masses of humanity and be a nonconformist intellectually and spiritually. When others are saying there is no God or that God doesn't matter, or God isn't relevant. You are willing to stand up and say that God does matter and God is relevant and God is the center of my life.

"Be ye transformed by the renewing of your mind; let this mind be in you that was in Christ Jesus."

It means that Christ dominates your intellectual and thinking processes because, you see, your mind was affected by sin, and that's why you cannot come to Christ with your intellect alone. You have to come by faith and when you do, He takes control of your mind.

"And I will keep him in perfect peace whose mind is stayed on thee."

We can have peace in the midst of a roaring, tension-filled world if our mind is on Him. It means that your intellect now has come under the Lordship of Jesus Christ. When you receive Christ as Savior you receive Him not just as Savior; you receive Him as Lord.

"Believe on the Lord Jesus Christ, and thou shalt be saved."

"If we confess with our mouths the Lord Jesus Christ," and believe that God has raised Him from the dead, we shall be saved.

The Lordship of Christ means that you not only receive Christ tonight as Savior from sin, but when you come, you must also receive Him as Lord. He takes over control of your life. He dominates your thinking processes —the things you read, the things you watch. Christ has a voice in it, and He has a decisive voice, and you discipline your mind for study and reading and learning about Him.

And then you're not to be conformed physically. You see, when you receive Christ your body becomes the temple of the Holy Spirit, and your body is presented as a living sacrifice to God. Your hands become His hands. Your eyes cannot look upon things that would displease Him. Do you want Him seeing through your eyes some of the things you look at today? Our ears, our feet, our entire body, surrendered to the Lordship of Christ.

We are not to be conformed to this world, religiously. We don't live by the world's definition of what it means to be religious.

People of Isaiah's day were very religious, but God said, "Bring no more vain oblations. Incense is an abomination unto me. The new moons and the Sabbath, the calling of assemblies, I cannot away with. It is iniquity, even the solemn meetings." He said, "Even your church services have become a sin to me. Get away with them."

Do you see, to be religious has one meaning today in America, but to be a Christian has a different meaning. You say, "I come from a Christian home. I was reared in a Christian country. I have Christian surroundings. I have Christian influences. I have gone to church all my life. Well, that makes me a Christian."

No, that does not make you a Christian. That does not make you a disciple of Jesus Christ. You must come under the Lordship of Christ. You must be born again. You must repent of sin. You must be converted. You must have a personal relationship with Christ, and if you don't have that personal relationship with Christ, you cannot be His follower. And it is a daily experience. It's not just coming forward in a Crusade like this one time. It is a daily experience. You come forward just as a start.

No, we're not to be conformed to this world. We don't hear much preaching and teaching today about separation, but I want to tell you that the time has come to start preaching and teaching what the Bible has to say about the world and the need of separation from the world. "Love not the world," says Scripture, "neither the things that are in the world." That word is "cosmos." That means the system of evil in the world. That doesn't mean the earth; that doesn't mean people; that means the system of evil of which the Bible says, "the devil is the prince of this world, the prince of the cosmos, he's the god of this cosmos. The 'cosmos' lies in the arms of the wicked one, this system of evil in this world, with all its implications from which we are to be separated," the Scripture says.

Now I can go out among publicans and sinners and I can go out to all of these different places. Jesus was accused of being a winebibber and a glutton and all kinds of things. He went to parties, but He never compromised with the evil He found there. He was among them, but not of them. We are to be in the world, but not of the world. We are citizens of two worlds. Christ lives in our hearts, and we are not to participate in the evils of this world. We are to live a life separated from the evils of this world. Jesus said, "Take heed to yourselves, lest at any time your heart be overcharged with eating too much and drunkenness and the cares of this life so that day comes upon us unawares." What day? The day of judgment, the day Christ is coming. He said He's going to come like a thief in the night. It's going to be like a thunderbolt and it could take us unaware.

The Apostle Peter said in 1 Peter 2:11, "Abstain from fleshly lusts which war against your soul." These fleshly lusts that are all about us have declared war against your spirit, against your spiritual life and against your relationship to God. A warfare takes place.

Now before you receive Christ, you have a nature dominated by self. When you receive Christ as Savior He gives you a "new nature." The "old nature" is still there, the "new nature" now comes in your heart to dwell. You yield the new nature to Christ as Lord and Master. He so dominates that "self" no longer sits on the throne. Sin and self shall no longer have dominion over you. God is now in control over your life, but a warfare constantly exists in the heart of a Christian. If you are a true believer of Christ, you are going to be at war. The lusts of the flesh, the world, and the devil are going to war against your Christian life. The flesh will lust against the spirit and the spirit against the flesh, and there will be a constant conflict. And the only time you have total peace is when you are totally committed and totally yielded in every phase of your life to Christ. Too many young people want to have one foot in the world and one foot in the kingdom of God, and it is like straddling a fence. You are not happy either way. Declare yourself. Get on one side or the other. Don't drag the name of Christ down by calling yourself a Christian and then living like the devil. You are doing more harm and it is better to get out of the church. Don't call yourself a Christian, if you're not one. In the early church they had some discipline in the church. If a man didn't live up to the Christian ethics, he was thrown out of the church. I will tell you what we need in America today is some backdoor revival meetings to get rid of some of the people we've got in the church. I believe we could do a better job if we were dedicated, disciplined disciples such as they had in the early church. It takes discipline to get up an hour earlier to study your Bible every morning. It takes discipline to turn off the television set an hour earlier in the evening in order to spend an hour in prayer. It takes the discipline that Job had when he said, "I have esteemed the words of his mouth more than my necessary food."

The Apostle Paul said, "But those things that were gain to me, those I counted loss for Christ. Yea, doubtless that I count all things but loss for the excellency of the knowledge of Christ Jesus my Lord for whom I have suffered the loss of all things."

And then Paul must have laughed. He said, "I count them but refuse and trash that I may win Christ." He said, "All the glory of this world, all the intellectualism I've had, all the money that I could have, I'd gladly give it up. It's trash compared to what I've found in Jesus Christ."

As Tom Skinner said tonight, "Old things pass away." The whole world becomes new, and Christ dominates our lives and dominates our thinking. The time has come to separate the men from the boys in the church. The time has come to ask young people to follow Jesus Christ, even if it means suffering; because that's what it means and that's what it will cost.

You know they placed an ad in *The New York Times*

some years ago. A man was going up to the Arctic—Shackleton, I believe. He placed an ad in *The New York Times* because he couldn't get any volunteers, and he said, "The pay is going to be low, and it's going to be tough, and it's going to be rough, and you may get killed," and do you know I believe I read that they had the largest response to that ad of any ad ever carried in *The New York Times?* Young people want a challenge. They want something tough and rough and that's what Jesus offers. He doesn't offer a good time. Jesus offers suffering. He offers a Cross. He offers death, but the rewards are fantastic—eternal life, peace and joy here. A supernatural power to love your friends and your neighbors. A new power to help the world in which we live by changing it for the better.

"Deny self and take up the Cross." What did He mean by the Cross? Now it's voluntary. You have a free choice. You don't have to take it up if you don't want to. Now it's not the Cross of punishment for sin. Christ alone could bear that. It's not a Cross of gold, of ivory and silver. It is not poverty and sickness. It is not the vexations of life. It is not the burdens you bear. Paul's Cross was not the thorn that he bore in the flesh. What did Jesus mean when he said, "Take up the Cross"? The Cross in that day was the place where they executed criminals. It would be as if I stood here tonight and said, "Take up your electric chair and follow Me." Why, you'd laugh. That's what they did in Jesus' day. In fact, most of the people turned and followed Him no more. They said, "Oh, we didn't know He was going to the Cross." Only a handful stuck with Him, but what a handful! Within a short time they changed the world.

Jesus said, "If you are going to follow Me, you are going to have to share the fellowship of My rejection."

"Yea, and all that live godly in Christ Jesus shall suffer persecution."

In Hebrews, the 13th chapter, it says, "Let us go forth therefore unto him without the camp, bearing his reproach. For here we have no continuing city, but we seek one to come."

"Bearing his reproach." That means going back to your address, back to your crowd and your gang and your school and saying, "Christ, I'm finished with the old life. I am going to live a new life." Then to turn around and walk out sharing the reproach of Christ not knowing when a knife could be thrust in your back or a bullet in your brain.

See, that's what God is calling on all of us to do in our own way, in our own sphere—to live for Christ even if you must stand alone. You may be the only one in your community, in your school. Like Noah in his generation. He was the only one. And there was a fellow in the Bible who came to Jesus and wanted to follow Him, and Christ said, "Young man, have you counted the cost?" Jesus said, "It is going to cost you everything." The young fellow said, "Well, Lord, I want to follow You, but I can't give up everything." Jesus said, "Nothing doing," and he lost that young fellow. The young fellow turned away grieved. And I want to tell you that if you're not willing to go all out for Jesus Christ and give Him all you've got, you will not be considered a follower of Him. But if you mean, if you want Him to dominate your life, and you want Him to be Lord and Savior, I'm going to ask you to receive Him tonight. Will you follow Christ tonight in a disciplined life, in a life of prayer, a life of Bible study, a disciplined mind, a crucified tongue, redeeming the time?

Lenin once said that a Communist is a dead man on furlough.

Winston Churchill once said, "There is so much to do in the world and so little time to do it."

You've got a lifetime before you. We don't know how long—maybe a year, two years, five years, ten years—you don't have long. Are you willing to give what you've got to Christ? You can come just as you are, with all your sins, all of your troubles, with all of your difficulties, come and say, "Lord Jesus, I receive you as my Lord and as my Savior. I want to be a follower of Yours. I want to be a true disciple."

I am going to ask you to get out of your seats and to come. If you've never received Christ as your Savior—or maybe you made a commitment at one time, but it really didn't mean much to you—I am going to ask you to come.

Delivered June 19, 1969

VIII.
TWO SETS OF EYES

I'm going to ask that we bow in prayer. Every head bowed and every eye closed in prayer. That song, sung by Norma Zimmer, is exactly right—"Only Believe." The question in many hearts and many minds—what does it mean to believe? That's a tricky little word. Your future destiny and eternity will depend on whether you believe or not, and you're not sure what the word "believe" means. If I were you, I would look it up in a dictionary. I'd look up the word "faith" because the Bible says that without faith it's impossible to please God. Our entire confidence in Christ is involved in that word "faith." What does it mean? It means commitment, to have confidence in, to put your trust in. And tonight I'm going to ask you to believe, to commit, to surrender the citadel of your soul, your will, to Christ. Say tonight, "I will follow Him. I will serve Him."

Our Father and our God, we pray that thy Holy Spirit will be speaking while I'm speaking, using the Word of God which is living and powerful and sharper than a two-edged sword. May people be conscious of Jesus tonight and not of the speaker. For we ask it in His name. Amen.

Now tonight I want you to turn with me to the third chapter of the book of Revelation, and the 17th verse. "Because thou sayest that I am rich, and increased with goods, and have need of nothing; and knowest not that thou art wretched, and miserable, and poor, and blind, and naked." You see, from our point of view, we look at things from one perspective, but God looks at us entirely differently. We look on the outward appearance; God looks on the inward appearance. God looks upon the heart. And when God looks upon the heart of all the people in America, in our affluency, many of us saying, "I am rich. I don't have a need of anything," God answers back and says, "You don't seem to realize that spiritually you're poor and blind and naked."

Now Dr. Hildebrand just a few moments ago read the story from the 10th chapter of Mark, of a blind man who encountered Jesus. This man was blind, and I would like to talk about that man and how he met Christ and how it changed his life and how you can meet Christ and He can change your life tonight.

In *The New York Times* this morning there was a beautiful picture of Tricia Nixon, and a blind boy was feeling her face to see what she looked like with the touch of his fingers. Tonight as I came in I saw a blind couple. They're the same couple I've seen a couple of nights and one night I looked over there—they look as though they're in their seventies—and they were holding hands, both of them blind.

I have a friend down in Florida who went blind suddenly at a rather young age, and he said, "I'm glad I'm blind because, since I've become blind I see so much better." What he meant was that he saw the real things of life so much better.

Helen Keller once said, "I have walked with people whose eyes are full of light but who see nothing. They see nothing in the woods or men or sky, nothing in the struggle, nothing in books, nothing in sports, nothing on the street. Their soul's voyage through this enchanted world is a barren waste."

And the prophet Isaiah once said, "They have eyes to see but they see not. They have ears to hear but they hear not."

TWO SETS OF EYES

Did you know that there's a great fantastic spiritual world that we've never seen with our physical eye?

Dr. Engstrom, who is chairman of the Executive Committee of RCA, had some of the Team members to lunch yesterday. He's chairman of this Crusade and he's a great scientist. And we got to talking about the possibility of another world on this planet that we're not conscious of and certainly the Bible teaches precisely that. But the interesting thing is that science is now on the threshold and is beginning to glimpse this other world through scientific instruments. The Bible tells us there is a world of evil and a world of good, a world with demons and a world with angels.

And when Elisha the prophet was under attack and the armies of Sennacherib were coming after him, his servant came in very agitated and disturbed and frightened, and said, "Elisha, they've come to get you and they're going to kill you." And Elisha sat in his rocking chair very relaxed and said, "Lord, open his eyes." And the eyes of the servant were opened and round about the mountain, the Bible tells us, was an army of angels with drawn swords to protect Elisha. And the armies of Sennacherib never came.

Do you see? There's an unseen world out there and there's an unseen world of joy and happiness and peace and security and fulfillment that you've never found because you've never had this spiritual experience, this encounter with Jesus Christ.

Now this man in our little story tonight was a blind man. His name was Bartimaeus. And do you remember reading a few days ago an American tourist was killed down on the Dead Sea—at a tourist resort in Israel when some bombs came in? Well not far from that very place is the little town of Jericho on the Jordan. You go down from Jerusalem and there is Jericho with its palm trees. And in this little town of Jericho was a man by the name of Bartimaeus. It was a cold spring morning, and he'd been sleeping in somebody's barn. He got up, and made his way with his cane down the street, begging a crust of bread here and there. He came to the outside of the town on the main road that went through Jericho to Jerusalem and sat down at the gate, at the city wall, and began to beg. He said, "Help the blind! Help the blind! Help the blind!" And people came by. Some of them spit at him, some threw rocks at him, some kicked him, some tossed a little coin. And the other beggars were there. They were competing for what little bit they might get, just enough to eke out an existence.

And I want you to look at this blind man for a moment and see his needs. The Bible says he was blind. He couldn't see the rags and the filth, nor could he see beauty. The Bible teaches that you and I have two sets of eyes. Your physical eyes may have 20/20 vision, but your spiritual eyes may be blinded. In fact, the Bible teaches that we have been blinded by a supernatural power. The Scripture says in 1 Corinthians 2:14, "But the natural man (that's the ordinary man) receiveth not the things of the Spirit of God for they are foolishness unto him; neither can he know them, because they are spiritually discerned."

The Bible says in 2 Corinthians 4:4, "In whom the god of this world hath blinded the minds of them which believe not, lest the light of the glorious gospel of Christ, who is the image of God, should shine unto them."

In other words there's a supernatural veil over our minds and over our spiritual eyes, and that's why a person can never come to Christ or to God by intellect alone. The Gospel just doesn't make sense. You'll never be able to figure it out logically step by step because sin has affected your thinking processes. Your normal intellectual life is conformed to this materialistic, secular world. And that's why the Gospel is "foolishness," the Bible says. The Bible says the preaching of the Cross is "foolishness" to them that perish.

Now that word "foolish" is a very interesting word in Greek. It means moron, idiotic. To the average person, for me to stand up here and proclaim that Christ died on the Cross, that He rose again; and that if you believe it and accept it, it could change your life, is idiotic. It's foolish. And God has done that deliberately.

TWO SETS OF EYES

I'll tell you why He's done it deliberately. You remember in the Old Testament there was a general by the name of Naaman and he was the commander-in-chief of the armies of Syria and he had leprosy. He couldn't get it cured. So he went over to see Elijah the prophet and the prophet said, "Go and dip seven times in the Jordan," and the great general left in a huff. He was angry. He said, "The waters of Syria are better than the waters of Israel. Why should I do such a foolish thing? There's no medical power in the waters of the Jordan." No. Elijah had told him to do something very foolish and very ridiculous in order to test his faith. You see, he had to go dip in that water by faith. Do something foolish—foolish to the natural mind, but not foolish to God. Obedience is important. God was teaching obedience.

Finally, one of his captains persuaded him to do it and he dipped seven times and he was cured of his leprosy.

Or do you remember the story Jesus told—and it's a big story in the Old Testament—about the serpent in the wilderness? You remember the snakes had bitten the people of Israel and many of them were dying. God said, "If you want to be cured, Moses, I want you to build a brazen serpent, a serpent of bronze, and everybody that looks at that serpent will live. Those that do not look will die."

Now isn't that ridiculous? There's no medical power in a serpent of bronze. Can you think of anything more ridiculous for a person who is bitten by a snake than to look at a bronze serpent and be healed? God was telling them to do something foolish. By faith! He wanted them to believe it because He said it. He was teaching obedience. Samuel said, "Obedience is better than sacrifice."

Well, that's the same thing about the Cross. The Cross is foolishness for the natural man. The whole first chapter of 1 Corinthians talks about the foolishness of the Cross to the logical intelligent mind. But when you come by faith as a little child to receive Christ, it takes on a new meaning, a new dimension. God has put His power locked up in the secret of the Cross. That's why every Catholic church has a Cross. That's why every Protestant church has a Cross. That's why the Cross is the symbol of Christianity. Because in the Cross there is a supernatural power to change your life. Now it looks foolish, it looks ridiculous to the natural mind, but there's power to change your life.

Now this man was blind, but so are many of you tonight. *Secondly, he was poor*. He was a very poor man. And you know that's a problem that we face in our world today. The problem of poverty. It causes an ache in my heart constantly. Seven out of 10 persons in the world are living in grinding poverty at this moment. Even before Biafra, 10,000 people were dying of starvation and malnutrition every day in the world. Think of it, 10,000 people a day dying of malnutrition in our world. And the pet dogs, our animal friends, in America, have a far higher standard of living than millions of people in other parts of the world.

And you know the Bible teaches that we have a responsibility to the poor. Proverbs 21:13 says, "Whosoever stoppeth his ears at the cry of the poor, he also shall cry himself but shall not be heard." Psalm 41:1 says, "Blessed is he that considereth the poor. The Lord will deliver him in trouble." Isaiah said, "Learn to do well, seek judgment, relieve the oppressed, judge the fatherless, plead for the widow." The Apostle John said, "Whosoever hath this world's goods and seeth his brother hath need and shutteth up his bowels of compassion. How can the love of God dwell in him?"

Well you'd say, "Billy, who are the poor in America?" We have right here on Manhattan Island the extreme rich and the extreme poor. Now according to the standards that they've laid out as to what is poverty in America they are poor. I was reared in real poverty. I didn't know it. Nobody came along and told me. I didn't watch a television program and see what a great problem I had become. Nobody told me. All I knew to do was to go out and work from three o'clock in the morning till sundown because for about seventeen years I thought that P.C. meant "Plow Corn," instead of "Preach Christ." At least my father thought it. I wasn't necessarily convinced of it but he was, and my brother and I, before we went to high school, had to get up and milk about twenty cows each every morning. Now you say, "That's impossible." I'd hate to have to milk one right now. But that was hard work.

And did you know we didn't have a television set? And we didn't have a radio until I was about twelve and my father bought an old crystal set and we put the earphones on and tuned in to KDKA in Pittsburgh. That was the only station on the air, I believe, at that time that we could get.

And we didn't have all the inside plumbing. Now we were in real poverty compared to today's standards. But we didn't know it. But there are really poor people in America—widows, children from broken homes, illegitimate children, orphans, the disabled, the old whose savings are being eaten away by inflation, those who want work but who are discriminated against because of race or religion. To all of those people society has a responsibility and the church has a very special responsibility.

I saw a sign the other day that said, "I fight poverty. I work." But I find a lot of people who don't really want to work, and the Bible says in 2 Thessalonians 3:10, "If any will not work, neither should he eat." Now that's not true of thousands, of hundreds of thousands, or perhaps millions, but it's true of some. And you know today it's hard to find people who want to work with their hands. Jesus was a carpenter. He worked with His hands. He was called a servant. But today we think that's below our dignity. Everybody wants to be an executive. Everybody wants to have an air-conditioned office, and I don't blame them. But somebody's got to work, and there's a dignity in working with your hands. There's a dignity to cleaning the street. There's a dignity to carrying the garbage. Don't be ashamed of that. If you're a Christian, you can throw your shoulders back and say, "Yes, sir, I'm a garbage collector and I'm proud of it." There's a dignity in being a maid. Any service, however lowly you may think it is, or however lowly other people think it is, in God's sight has a dignity to it.

Jesus was a carpenter. And the Scripture says in Ephesians, "Let him labor, working with his hands the thing which is good, that he may have to give to him that needs it."

Now there are some people who have a great burden for poverty and that's fine. We all have a burden for poverty, or we should, as Christians. But you know Judas had a great burden for the poor because when Mary Magdalene came in and anointed the feet of Jesus and washed His feet with her hair and poured some expensive ointment, Judas was angry. And he said, "Lord, why didn't we take this money that's been thrown away on your feet and give it to the poor?" And the Bible has an interesting comment—John 12:6, listen. "Judas was not concerned with the poor because he was a thief. He wanted it for himself." And many politicians carry a heavy burden for poverty because they want votes.

But that should never do away with our responsibility for the legitimate poor. We as a society, and we as a church, should do all we can for the poverty-stricken.

But there's another kind of poverty the Bible says. There's a spiritual poverty. "A little that a righteous man hath is better than the riches of many wicked." The Bible says, "What shall it profit a man if he gain the whole world and lose his own soul."

And Jesus told the story of a rich man. This was an affluent man. He had everything. And one day he went out and looked over his estate and said, "You know I've got enough to retire on. I'm going to go down to Florida to spend the rest of my life. I've got big barns. I've got big estates." And he said to his soul—he didn't say to his mind or to his body—he said to his soul, his spirit, that part of him that should have belonged to God—he said, "Soul, take thine ease and drink and be merry. Go have a good time. Enjoy yourself."

Now this was selfishness. Don't go help others, don't get involved in social enterprises and spiritual work and witnessing, but spend it on yourself. And that night, the Bible says, there came a voice from heaven saying, "Thou fool, this night is thy soul required of thee."

TWO SETS OF EYES

Amos in the sixth chapter says, "Woe to them that are at ease, that lie upon beds of ivory and stretch themselves up on their couches and eat the lambs out of the flock and the calves out of the midst of the stall. That drink wine in bowls and anoint themselves with the cheap ointments." The fall of Rome came about three ways—gluttony, drunkenness, and immorality—that ate the heart and the core of Rome out. And these are the things we see in America tonight, that could cause us to rot from the inside unless we have a moral and a spiritual awakening from coast to coast.

But there's a spiritual poverty. You see, this man that Jesus told about had everything materially, but he had nothing spiritually. He had gained the world, but he lost his soul, and Jesus said that's a poor bargain. And some of you have a good job, you have a bank account, and you have a standing in your particular sphere, but spiritually you're poor. In God's sight you're in poverty. You're like Bartimaeus, blind and poor.

And then Bartimaeus was not only blind and poor, but he was in *a hopeless condition*. You see he'd tried to find a cure for his disease of blindness but he couldn't. And how many people here tonight are the same way? The pressures of life are pressing in, and it seems almost hopeless. A lot of you young people try to find a purpose and a meaning in your lives. You've tried to find the answers to the mysteries of life. Where did I come from? Why am I here? Where am I going? What's life all about?

The late Ian Fleming, the author and creator of James Bond, said before his death, "I'm now, my God, ashes, just ashes. You have no idea how bored one gets with the whole silly business of life." And psychologists are calling it "the suicide mentality" and they're now saying that the higher the civilization, the higher the suicide rate.

Bartimaeus expected to die in his blindness, never dreaming that something would happen to change his life. He had no ray of hope. And many of you have given up, and you're like the cat that had its tail stepped on so many times, that every time someone came in the room he stuck it out. You just say, "Well, there's no use. I've tried, I've tried religion, I've tried this church and that church and the other church; and I've tried philosophy and I've tried psychology." Even the Beatles went over to India searching for satisfaction and peace but they came back disillusioned. You've tried a thousand ways to find peace of soul and security of soul, but you haven't found it and so you've sort of given up.

Well, we've got a pretty dangerous situation developing in the world right now. Many of our great scientists are saying we'll never reach the twenty-first century. A Canadian physicist said the other day that man now has the power, if applied in its maximum dosage, to cause the world and all in it to disintegrate in less than one minute. We live on the brink of total annihilation—in the shadow of all that's happening all over the world—you see, we're living in a world controlled by sin, dominated by sin, so we have to keep strong defenses.

This is what Joel said. He said, "Proclaim ye this among the nations. Prepare for war, wake up the mighty men. Let all the men of war draw near, let them come up. Beat your plow shares into swords and pruning hooks into spears. Let the weak say 'I'm strong.' "

Jesus said there would be wars and rumors of wars till the end of time. We might as well face the fact that there's going to be war. There have been 51 wars since the end of World War II. We're heading toward what may be a gigantic conflict unless somehow the human race can have an intervention by God—and that's precisely what's going to happen. I'll talk about that Sunday night—when God intervenes to save us because God is going to end all this, and Jesus Christ His Son is going to come back and set up His Kingdom. That's the picture of Utopia that the world is dreaming of now and hoping for. But it will not come by the efforts of man. It is going to come by the intervention of God.

But you see spiritually we're all hopeless. Many of you realize it. You've been searching for a way out of your situation. And Bartimaeus was sitting there that morning blind, and poor, and hopeless and all of a sudden he heard a crowd coming down the road—boys whistling,

TWO SETS OF EYES

people laughing, and he said, "Who's coming?" Nobody answered. He said again, "I say, who's coming?" He couldn't get an answer in the confusion and the crowd was beginning to pass him by, and so he grabbed for the skirt of a passerby and said, "Who's coming?" and this stranger jerked away and said, "Jesus of Nazareth passeth by." "Jesus of Nazareth. I've heard that name. Why, Jesus is the one who's been doing all these miracles. I've heard about him."

Now Bartimaeus would have never heard had it not been for a stranger who just gave him a word. You never know what one word in a restaurant, on an elevator, on a street corner, will do. Many of you don't know, but you can go out to Central Park and we have meetings there during the day, and on Times Square, down in Greenwich Village at night, and Washington Square. In all these places, meetings are going on all day long. We have nearly two hundred people here with us. University students, evangelists from Africa, from Latin America, from Europe, helping us in this Crusade and the meeting here is just one of many meetings held all day long throughout New York.

Well yesterday these wonderful Italian fellows, the Palermo brothers, were out on the street and they were singing and they were giving their message, and a fellow sat up in an apartment building and listened. He called in today and said, "Those boys didn't know it, but I was in desperate condition and I received Christ into my heart." And he came here last night and came forward to make his decision publicly.

Another fellow rushed out of a building where one of our fellows was preaching and said, "My God, I've got to have God. I've got to have Him now." And he found God right on the street corner.

That's happening all over this city. You never read about it or hear about it but it's going on. One of our fellows was preaching and a fellow had a cobra, a snake from India. He pulled it out of a bag and held it up to his face to see if he'd flinch. He didn't flinch so the fellow stayed and listened to him preach.

We never know what one word will do. The secretary of the YMCA in Berlin, Germany, is Peter Schnieder, and he is always my interpreter when I go to Germany. Peter Schnieder was captured by the British during the war. He was in the German army. He learned English while he was in a British prison camp. After the war the YMCA chose him as a promising youth leader and brought him to this country to show him the various camps in this country to try to train him. And he was taken to Green Lake, Wisconsin. He was only a professing Christian; he didn't have any real faith. And there was nothing to do and so some student group was having a Christian meeting and he attended, and listened. And after the service a student came up to him and said, "Aren't you the young man from Germany?" He said, "Yes." He said, "Do you know Christ as your Savior?" and Peter Schnieder said, "What do you mean? Of course I'm a Christian. Everybody in Germany is a Christian." And he argued and debated and this went on about an hour, and, finally, he just turned around and walked away, angry.

He said he couldn't sleep all night, and for three days and three nights God spoke to him, and finally he got down beside his bed in another town and gave his life to Christ. He said, "Ever since then, every time I come to America, I look out across the audience to see if I can see that young man who faithfully witnessed to me that night, but I've never been able to find him, nor thank him. He probably left thinking he had lost his fish, that he'd been a failure in his witness, but," Peter Schnieder said, "I'll see him in heaven some day and I'll be able to thank him for leading me to the knowledge of Jesus Christ."

You see, when you witness for Christ and they say "No," if you've been faithful, God will have planted a seed.

The Surgeon General of one of the countries of Europe was walking down the street one day and a piece of paper stuck to his shoe. He went in, took it off, and it was a Gospel tract that somebody had faithfully given out. He read it, he was converted, and today he is a Christian leader.

TWO SETS OF EYES

You see, Jesus was passing by and right now Jesus is passing by in New York. Jesus was passing by in Jericho and in desperation Bartimaeus could have said, "Now wait a minute. I think I'll wait for the religious leaders to tell me about this Jesus fellow." But he didn't do that. He didn't wait until he could find out more. He said, "This is my one big moment," and he yelled at the top of his lungs, "Jesus, Jesus, have mercy on me." And the Bible says that Jesus stopped. Think of it now. This was the last time Jesus was ever in Jericho. He was already almost out of earshot and Bartimaeus was taking this one opportunity that might never come his way again, and he cried, "Jesus, have mercy on me," and Jesus stopped.

And let me tell you this. If you call on Him tonight, He'll stop and He'll listen to you. And the other beggars around Bartimaeus began to hit him in the mouth and saying, "Shhh! Shut up! He doesn't want to fool with an old dirty beggar like you—an old blind man."

Jesus didn't come to be ministered to. He came to minister and He's interested in you. And He has the hairs of your head numbered and He knows all about you. He knows the façade of religion, He knows the hypocrisy in your heart, or He knows the pride that you have, or He knows the lust of your heart, or He knows the habit that has a grip on you. He knows about that dope. He knows about all of those things. He knows about the relationships with your family that are under tension. He knows all about these conflicting things in your life and He says, "I love you. I want to forgive you, I want to help you. I'll stop whatever I'm doing to listen to you no matter who you are."

And Jesus said, "Call him." The other beggars could hardly believe it. They said, "Bartimaeus, He's calling you." And Bartimaeus could hardly believe it himself. And they gave him his coat, they gave him his cane, and he threw them both away and ran to Jesus and knelt down in front of Him. And there you have the man that's blind and helpless and poor, face to face with The Son of the living God. What an encounter! There's a picture of the human race. There's a picture of you, face to face with Jesus.

And Jesus asked Bartimaeus, "What do you want me to do? How can I help you?" Now, of course, Bartimaeus was blind and Jesus knew that. And Dr. Steven Olford gave me a wonderful thought a moment ago. He said the reason Jesus asked that question is because Bartimaeus had so adjusted to his blindness and his poverty and his helplessness, Jesus wanted to know if he really wanted to be changed. He wanted to see if he would accept the responsibility of being whole. "Bartimaeus, are you willing to adjust to a whole new life?" Did you know that there are a lot of people who love their sins so much they don't want to give them up. They love their condition so much they like to complain about it. I've met people who are sick. They enjoy their sickness. They enjoy telling you about it. They enjoy complaining. They enjoy the attention it gives them.

And this was the question I think that Jesus was asking Bartimaeus: "What do you want me to do? Bartimaeus, do you really want to be changed?" And Bartimaeus said a wonderful word in Greek. He said, "Lord." At that moment he said, "My Lord, my own Lord, that I may receive my sight." And Jesus said, "Bartimaeus, your sins are forgiven. You're made whole. Go your way." And the Scripture says that immediately his eyes opened. Notice, immediately! You ought to pick up the New Testament sometime and study this. The people who met Jesus, most of them, just met Him for an instant, or a moment, or an hour. But they were never the same after that. A miracle happened immediately, just like that, suddenly.

That night in the book of Acts when the Apostle Paul was in jail, and the earthquake came and the walls came tumbling down, the jailer was frightened and terrified, and he fell down before Paul and said, "What must I do to be saved?" Paul didn't give him some complicated answer. He didn't give him a long list of rules and regulations. All Paul said was, "Believe on the Lord Jesus Christ and thou shall be saved and thy house."

Very simple. Why, I'm sure that we would have taken

him to a psychiatrist and the psychiatrist might have said, "You're in no emotional state to make a decision like that. Your emotions have been aroused by this earthquake." But Paul didn't say that. He said, "Believe on the Lord Jesus Christ," and that night Paul baptized him, that night he entered the church, that night his life was changed.

That can happen to you tonight and you can start following Christ as Bartimaeus did. Would you like Christ to come into your life? And forgive your sins? And give you spiritual riches? And give you the certainty that you're going to heaven if you die? You can have that encounter.

Now, you see, when you come to Christ, that's only the first step and it's not easy to follow Him. It means persecution, suffering, self-denial and Cross bearing, but it's a challenge and it's a cause to commit your life to. And we have seen thousands of young and old alike make that commitment since we've been in New York. To let Him touch your life and change you and give you a reason for living is wonderful! It will give you the fulfillment and the certainty that you've been searching for. And then when you leave here you don't leave alone. Christ goes to live with you, back to the same old address, the same old crowd, the same old street. But it'll all look new to you after you've met Jesus.

I'm going to ask you tonight to receive Him, simply, by faith. Notice He said, "Thy faith hath made thee whole." Not your intellectual comprehension, but your faith. And Jesus said you have to become as a little child and receive Christ.

I'm going to ask you to get up out of your seat, hundreds of you, and come and stand in front of this platform and say by so coming, "I receive Christ. I want Him to forgive my sin and change my life."

And after you've all come and stood here a moment, I'm going to say a word to you and have a prayer with you and give you some literature and you can go back and join your friends. From that top gallery up there that we can see from here, you get up and go back and around. All the others can come straight down on the floor. And you in the other auditoriums who are watching at the Forum and the Manhattan Center, get up out of your seat and come forward in your auditorium to receive Christ, as many people are already beginning to come here. And after you've all come we're going to wait and have a prayer.

Delivered June 20, 1969

IX.
THE GIANTS YOU FACE

Now tonight I want to speak primarily to young people. I read today that many people are confused and discouraged about the relationship of colleges, universities, high schools and grammar schools throughout the country. Teachers are afraid of the principal and the principal is afraid of the superintendent. The superintendent is afraid of the school board, and the school board is afraid of the parents, and the parents are afraid of the young people, and the young people are not afraid of anybody. I think that is about the way it is most everywhere today.

But you know there is something else happening today. The suicide rate among teenagers in New York City has quadrupled. A Pennsylvania State University junior jumped to his death this past year. A Protestant minister went with his parents to get his belongings out of his dormitory room. They found there scrawled across the wall this slogan: "Life is hell."

How different from the story on the front page of the second section of *The New York Times* today—Dr. Kenneth Pike making the statement that two thousand tribes around the world still do not have the Bible, or portions of the Bible, translated into their languages and are asking young people to come into Wycliffe Bible Translators and help them translate the Bible in these languages around the world. And already many young people are out translating the Scriptures, living in tribal areas all through Latin America, in New Guinea, and with scores of other tribes and nations. What a challenge! There are thousands of challenges today. I wish that I were twenty years younger and I wish that I were twenty people, and could do all I would like to do. The challenge is greater than ever before for a young person who means business with Christ.

And you know I think it is good that we Christians are becoming a small minority—those of us who really believe in Christ. That is how the early church turned the world upside down. I think there have been too many of us. We've gotten in each other's way, and we haven't had the discipleship and the dedication. What we need is a dedicated minority to change America and the world.

Now tonight I want to turn to 1 Samuel, the 17th chapter. I'm not going to read it to you, but I am going to tell you the story of a young man who gave his life to God at an early age. His name was David, and he eventually became the great king of Israel and one of the ancestors of Jesus Christ.

In 1 Samuel it says, "And all this assembly shall know that the Lord saveth not with sword and spear: for the battle is the Lord's, and he will give you into our hands [Meaning David's]." (1 Samuel 17:47)

I want to go into the picture of the battle that David had with Goliath. Do you remember that story? Goliath was the biggest man who ever lived, as far as we know. He was nine feet, four inches, and his clothes were his armor. His spear was heavier than an oak tree, and he defied the armies of Israel for forty days in the valley of Elah. The Philistines were on one side, the Israelites were on the other. He would come out every day, morning and afternoon, and laugh at the Israelites and defy them. He said, "Send me a champion. Send your strongest, your biggest man to fight me, and whoever wins will win the war. Whoever loses will lose the war." Now maybe that's the way we should do in modern warfare. That would be like President Thieu of South Vietnam challenging Ho Chi Minh in North Vietnam to a personal fight. Whoever won the fight would win the war. That would save a lot of trouble, a lot of money, and a lot of lives. Now I didn't mean that as a political declaration, but it might not be a bad idea. I tell you, we would have a lot fewer wars if that happened.

Goliath would come out every day, morning and afternoon, and say, "I defy the armies of Israel this day. Give me a man. Come on, you cowards. See if you can find a man who will come out and fight me." Forty days and forty nights he kept that up, and they were scared to death.

King Saul was a great giant of a man himself, but he was afraid. He would hide in his tent and try to plan strategy. "How in the world are we going to defeat this big giant of a man?"

Did you know that every one of us here tonight faces giants in his life? Today we call them "hangups," but they are giants that we face. The world faces the giants of poverty, racial tensions, inflation, war, population explosion —all of these are giants that we face in our world. But on the personal level, the average young person faces giant problems. How are you going to cope with them? How are you going to meet them? How are you going to defeat them? How do you handle your hangups?

Well, one of the giants that young people face—and are unconscious of—is the desire for acceptance, status, recognition, admiration.

I asked a teen-age boy the other day, "Why do you like to ride that motorcycle?" This was down in the little town where I live. He said, "Boy, when you come zooming up on this bike, the girls really look at you."

And that is why a lot of young people today are "doing their thing." Now we can interpret that in all kinds of ways. But it is a desire to be accepted, to be recognized; status-seeking.

And then secondly, there is another giant that you might not be conscious of—a big giant that you face in your life—and that is a longing for security. Now young people may be in rebellion, and most young people do go through a period in their lives, and in later adolescence when they rebel a little bit. Now their parents may or may not be conscious of it. However, most parents today *are* conscious of it. But there is a period when you begin to disassociate from your mother and your father a little, and there is a natural rebellion. Some of it becomes violent rebellion. If the parents handle it right and the young people know what is happening physiologically, psychologically, spiritually, philosophically, it will be rather a smooth transition. Most parents don't go into it enough or take time to understand, and it becomes a violent, radical rebellion.

But do you know that most young people want authority? I go to some universities and I go to some colleges where there are no rules. Everything is permissive, and you find the most miserable-looking, unhappy people. I've gone to other universities and colleges and seen a very different picture. Or let's take some of the military academies, like West Point or Annapolis. Ben Fairchild is on the platform. He was the senior chaplain in Vietnam when I was out there and handled our schedule when I was preaching to the troops two years ago. He will tell you, "They've got a thousand rules in those academies that in my judgment don't mean a thing. I asked, 'Why do you have so many rules on everything?' They said, 'We're teaching discipline.' "

And those young men coming from the finest homes in America are happy because they have authority and they have discipline because, you see, we were made for them. And that's why it is important to come under the authority of the Lordship of Christ. That's also why a lot of young people don't want Christ. They don't want to be told what to do.

Jesus said, "You can't serve two masters." You have to choose. Either serve yourself and go your own way.

All we like sheep have gone astray.

Or you serve him, Christ. He says, "There is no neutral ground. There is no middle road. You have to choose." Which road are you going to choose? Which life are you going to live? Are you going to live a life of self-centeredness, or are you going to live a life under the Lordship and authority of Jesus Christ? "Ye call me Lord and Master, and ye do well, for so I am," He said.

Then there is another giant young people face that they may not be conscious of either. That's the giant of the hunger to be loved. Freud said that's the greatest instinct that we have—this longing to be loved.

A juvenile judge said some time ago, "I've never had a wayward girl before me who was loved by her father."

A sixteen-year-old girl who had just had an illegitimate baby was quoted in the paper the other day as saying that teen-age girls engage in premarital sex because they don't get enough love at home and they think they are getting love that way.

You see, the Bible teaches that God loves you. God loves you so much that He gave His Son to die on the Cross for you. And with every drop of blood that Jesus Christ shed, He was saying, "I love you, I love you, I love you even to the death."

"No matter how bad you are, no matter what your sins are, I love you," says Christ.

And this longing to be loved, this longing to be accepted, this longing for status can all be met in a relationship with Jesus Christ. Give your life to Christ. He will give you a status and standing. You become a joint heir with Jesus Christ. You become a member of the royal family of heaven. He will meet that need to be loved because He loves you more than any friend, and more than your mother.

"I have loved you, saith the Lord. He that loveth Me shall be loved of my Father," says the Scripture.

Then, there is another giant that young people face in their lives today. That is the problem of sex—how to handle sex. And you know probably one of the best-known folk singers today is Sebastian Temple, who, by the way, is a very wonderful Christian, and he said some time ago, "Love is silence, lust is a roar. Love is a sacrifice; lust always wants more. Love is a giving; lust only takes. Love is a meeting of hearts; lust breaks."

Yes, the Bible has a lot to say about sex. It is not a hush-hush book on the subject. Sex is not sin. Lust is sin. Man has taken something good and holy and corrupted it. God's great gift has been perverted.

Why does God say, "Thou shalt not commit immorality outside of marriage"?

First, to protect your marriage.

Second, to protect your body. In spite of all of the modern drugs we have, there are more illegitimate children being born every day in this country, more venereal disease than at any time in American history right now. There are new strains of it coming from the Far East that do not respond to drugs, and it is sweeping the country.

God said that to protect you psychologically—because of the guilt feelings, the emotional disturbances, the insecurity, the feeling of not being loved—sex must be controlled.

I don't believe that you can live a life according to the Bible in which you flee youthful lusts and avoid the pitfalls of immorality without Jesus Christ. I believe the temptations are too great. I believe the pressures of our sex-saturated age are too great. I don't believe that you can do it, but if Christ is in your heart, He gives you a supernatural power to live a clean life.

You say, "But, Billy, at this point I have already broken God's law. What am I going to do?" He will forgive you. That's what the Cross is all about. That's why He died on the Cross for you. His blood can wash away any sin, whatever your sin may be. That's why He died for you. He loves you. He will forgive you and make you as clean and as pure as any virgin who ever lived if you put your confidence and your trust in Him. Is sex the giant in your life that you need some help on?

Paul wrote to Timothy and said, "Keep thyself pure." He said, "Flee youthful lusts." He said, "I keep my body under, and bring it into subjection to the Lordship of Christ."

Another giant that young people are facing today is the

giant of a vocation. What am I going to do with my life? How many young people waste so much of their life trying to decide? There are a thousand challenges today, a thousand things you can do for God. How many young people come to me and say, "I'm bored." A Christian young person should never be bored. There is the Bible to study; there are people to win; there is work to be done, there are the poor to be fed. And out on the mission fields of the world are frontiers of the Christian faith where you are needed. There is not a person here in my judgment who is not qualified to serve God in some way. Even on a hospital bed—you may be deaf or you may be dumb or you may be blind—God can use you if you offer yourself to Him. Many of you need to go and get training. You know, God uses only prepared people. Some of you need to go to Bible School or you need to go into some Christian group to study and prepare to serve Him.

And then there is the problem of temptation. What am I going to do with temptation? You know how Jesus overcame temptation? He just quoted Scripture; that's all He ever did.

"Thy word have I hid in my heart that I might not sin against thee," said David, and when he stopped quoting Scripture, temptation got to him.

When Jesus was tempted, He didn't argue with the devil; He just quoted the Bible. That's the reason we give you verses here every night to memorize because everybody is tempted every day. Now temptation is not a sin. It is yielding to the temptation that is a sin, and Jesus quoted Scripture to the devil, and the devil fled. The Bible says, "Resist the devil." How do you resist him? You resist him with the sword of the Spirit. The Bible is your weapon. It is a living Word. There is something supernatural about just quoting Scriptures. It is God's inspired Word, and that's the reason it is so important to memorize these verses and keep memorizing them so that when temptation comes, you can have a Scripture to quote, and the devil will flee.

So this giant Goliath was out challenging all the armies of Israel, and everybody was afraid. David was watching the sheep. He wasn't even old enough to go to war. His brothers had gone to fight. They weren't doing much fighting. They were just sitting around listening to a big giant brag, and they were all scared to death. So David's father came to him and said, "Son, I want you to go out to the armies and take some grain and some bread out there and give it to your brothers. They are probably hungry." So David went out with the bread and the grain and when he arrived there with these provisions, he heard this big giant. The ground almost shook at the power of his voice. He said, "I defy the armies of Israel. Send a man out here to fight me." And David said, "Who in the world is that fellow defying the armies of the Lord God? Who is that guy?" They said, "He's Goliath." They said, "He's the biggest man in the world; the most powerful man in the world."

David said, "Why doesn't someone go fight him?"

They said, "We're all scared. We'd never win. He'd kill us all."

David looked at him and said, "I'll fight him."

And his brothers laughed at him and sneered and mocked and the whole group of soldiers laughed.

"Huh, a boy like you going out to fight a giant like that? Are you crazy? Don't make a fool of yourself trying to show off."

He said, "Take me to King Saul. I volunteer to fight the giant."

So they took him to King Saul, and King Saul said, "Well, you're just a boy. I can't send you out there to fight Goliath. Why the greatest warriors we've got are afraid of him. He'll cut your head off with that giant sword of his."

David said, "Sir, your Majesty, out yonder while I was watching my sheep a bear came out. It killed the sheep. With my bare hands God helped me to kill the bear. A lion came out to grab one of our sheep one day, and God helped me to vanquish the lion with my bare hands. And the same God that helped me in the fight with the bear, and helped me in the fight with the lion is going to help me with the fight with Goliath because Goliath should not be allowed to defy the armies of the Lord God."

Saul said, "All right, if you are determined to go, go ahead. But you don't have any army, you don't have a sword, you don't have any weapons—here take mine."

So he clothed him in his own armor. Now David had a strong faith. It must have taken a lot of faith out there with that bear. We've got bears down where I live, and I wouldn't want to go out and face one of them. So it must have taken a lot of faith. Tarzan had a knife, but David didn't even have a knife when he faced that lion, but he whipped the lion. Now have you ever tried to beard a lion and wrestle with him? Well, that's what David did.

You see, his spiritual strength had been developed in secret and nourished in solitude. He had made his decision to live for God out under the stars and out on the desert, and he determined that he was going to serve God at an early age.

What a magnificent Psalm that was that was read a moment ago. David wrote it. Most of the Psalms were written by David, and many of them were written when he was a shepherd boy out under the stars at night just thinking about God. Now here in New York you can hardly see the stars at night. You have to look at them on television. When the astronauts are going around the moon, you get a view of the stars. But out on the solitude of the desert—I wonder if you ever get alone with God. Do you ever just get a chance to be alone with Him? You say, "Billy, are you kidding? With my five children, in our apartment, our flat, me get alone with God?"

I know a woman who had twelve children in a flat in London, and she said the way she got alone was just to take the apron and throw it over her head, and she'd stand there alone and pray.

You can get alone.

And then David had exercised—he had exercised his spiritual faith in lonely combat. You see nobody saw him fight that bear, and nobody saw him with that lion except God. He never dreamed the whole world would hear that story for generations to come. He didn't have to go, you

THE GIANTS YOU FACE 115

see, by the experience of somebody else. He had experienced God for himself.

And that's the trouble with young people today. They're waiting for a hand-me-down religion, and they have discarded Christianity because they say, "It hasn't worked in my parents' lives; my parents are big hypocrites. It didn't work for them."

You see, you have a caricature of Christianity. I'm not really asking you to come to Christianity as an institution. I'm asking you to have a personal relationship with Jesus Christ on your own—your own experience.

David had his own experience. He didn't depend on the faith of his father. He went on an experience that he himself had had with God. It had stood the test of daily life. You see, he led a disciplined life. He disciplined his mind; he disciplined his body; he disciplined his tongue; he disciplined his sex life. He learned to play the harp; he learned to write poetry. He didn't spend his time hanging around the bars, running around with gangs—he studied on his own. When his time came, God used him. He withstood the rebukes, the sneers and the mockings of his brothers and his friends. They laughed at him for the faith he had in God, just as they are going to laugh at you when you go back to school and back to your neighborhood and say, "I've become a Christian. I've received Christ." Some of your friends are going to drop you like a hot potato, and you will have to make new friends, but God will provide them. God will test you for a while as He did David. The bear may come; the lion may come, and God is going to say, "All right, here's the big test. I'll help you if you are willing to let Me help you." And God will help you in those tests, and when you come through, then the big test will come, then victory! You will be out on your own and you will find yourself with a thousand new friends whom you hadn't dreamed of all over the world who are your brothers and sisters. You talk about soul brothers—when you come to Christ you have got some soul brothers. Black becomes beautiful, and white is beautiful, and yellow is beautiful, and red is beautiful—it's all good when you come to Christ.

And then it withstood the rationalization of the intellect. You see, his mind might have played tricks on him, and he might have tried to figure it out because you see, Saul said, "Go out there in my armor. My armor has been in a hundred battles. I've got the finest sword in the world. Take it with you."

David clothed himself, and he could hardly move in all this armor. He couldn't fight in all that paraphernalia. You see, the Bible says, "For the weapons of our warfare are not carnal, but mighty through God to the pulling down of strongholds." The Bible says, "We wrestle not against flesh and blood, but against principalities, and against powers, and against the rulers of the darkness of this world, against spiritual wickedness in high places." You see, it is a spiritual conflict we are involved in. You can't go out there and train as you would for a championship fight. You train in a different way—weapons of the Spirit, prayer, Bible study, living a disciplined life for God. That's how you train for the great spiritual battles of life.

So David went out, and he did an interesting thing. He had a slingshot and he stopped at a brook and picked up five stones. Somebody asked why he had five stones; he only needed one. Someone has pointed out that Goliath had four relatives, and David had a stone for every one of them.

Now David was without experience. Goliath had more experience than he did. He was outnumbered because Goliath had his armor bearer. He was outarmed, he was outweighed, but David said, "You come to me with a sword. You come to me with a shield and a spear, but I come to you in the name of the Lord of Hosts. I come to you in God's name."

And the Bible says that he took that slingshot, he put a stone in it, and flung the stone at Goliath. The great giant had a look of surprise on his face; a thought entered his mind that had never been there before. That stone went right into his brain, and he crumpled and fell—dead. God had delivered the giant by the little David with a slingshot.

Now that story applies to you spiritually. There are many giants in your life. You've got some big giants, hangups. I want to tell you that with faith in Christ, with Christ in your heart, you can go out and you can defeat the biggest giant in the world. You can defeat that giant of sex. You can defeat that giant of wanting to be loved. You can defeat those giants that we mentioned a moment ago. Do you have a hangup with your parents? That can be overcome with Christ. Do you have a hangup with your friends or with loneliness, emptiness, no motivation? Give your life to Christ, serve Him—serve in His cause, and take five stones with you.

First, take a personal faith in Christ, which you can receive tonight.

Second, have a daily devotional life. Don't let a day go by without Bible-reading and prayer.

Third, lead a disciplined life under the Lordship of Christ.

Fourth, have a dedication to the service of others.

Fifth, be prepared.

Lincoln said one time, "I will prepare, and someday my chance will come."

And then when you throw the stone, God will direct it, for, you see, you won't have to go into battle alone; the Spirit of God will go with you.

And here's the glorious thing that I can never get over to the press: When you come to Christ, the Holy Spirit comes and takes up residence in your heart. Something new is added to your life supernaturally. A new power, a new dimension, a new ability to love, a new joy, a new peace—the Holy Spirit comes in and the Holy Spirit lives the Christian life through you. I know what you're saying. You're saying, "How in the world can I live that kind of a life? I'm not that good." Of course you're not; neither am I, but Christ can live through you if you let Him. All you have to do is get out of the way, take your hands off the controls of your life, and let Him do the controlling. Put Him at the controls, and you can handle any giant that comes along.

I am going to ask you to do that tonight. You say, "But

what do I have to do?" You have to be willing to repent of your sin—repent means to change, to change your mind, to turn from sin. It means saying, "Oh, God, I've sinned; I've failed; I'm sorry, forgive me. I am willing to change."

Secondly, it means receiving Christ as your Lord and your Savior, your only Savior, not trusting in your good works, not trusting even in your church membership, but trusting in the Person of Jesus Christ. In other words, having your own experience with Christ. It means you are willing to obey Him and serve Him and follow Him. Will you do that tonight? You may be a member of the church; you may not be a member of any church; but tonight you would like to receive Christ because you've got some giants in your life and you would like to have Christ help you. You would like Him to forgive your sins. You would like to receive Him as your Lord and your Savior, and you would like to leave here with Christ living in your heart. If you say that tonight and you want to do that—you may be Catholic, Protestant, or Jewish; you may not have any religion, but you want Christ in your heart—I want you to get up out of your seats all over the stadium and come and stand in front of this platform and say by coming, "I receive Christ. I want my sins forgiven. I want a new life."

Delivered June 21, 1969

X.

THE DAY TO COME

I'm going to ask that we bow our heads in prayer. There are hundreds of people here tonight in this great Garden who have problems that need to be solved, burdens that

THE DAY TO COME

need to be lifted, and sins that need to be forgiven. Many of you need a new dimension in your life, a new objective, a new meaning as to what life is all about. There's no purpose and direction in your life. You could find it on this last night of this great Crusade. Thousands of people during the past few days have had an encounter with Jesus Christ. Many of them will never be the same. You, too, can have an encounter with Christ this night.

The Bible says, "The summer is ended, the harvest is past, and we're still not saved." This particular harvest will be past in a few minutes, and many of you still have not met Christ. I hope that you'll not let this night pass till you have met Him face to face.

Our Father and our God, we pray that thy Holy Spirit will convince of sin and righteousness and judgment and thy Holy Spirit will draw men, women and young people to the Savior. For we ask it in His name. Amen.

Now tonight I want you to turn with me for the last sermon to the third chapter of 2 Peter. I want to speak tonight on the subject "The Signs of the Time," the end of the world, the second coming of Jesus Christ. And I want you to turn with me to the third chapter, beginning at verse 3 of 2 Peter. "Knowing this first, that there shall come in the last days. . . ." Now notice that expression "the last days." You'll find it many times in the Bible.

The Bible says that there is going to be an X point in history that will be known as the latter days or the last days. Many people think that we're in that period now. Nobody knows for sure. The Bible warns us against speculating on times and seasons and dates. But there is a period of time taught in the Bible that is called "the last days."

And the next word is "scoffers." Scoffers will come in the last days. Cynics. People who say, "Oh, yeah! God is dead. We can't find God anywhere. We took a trip up in space. We didn't meet God. We didn't meet any angels while we were up there." And there are going to be other scoffers who will scoff at the idea of future judgment, scoff at the idea that Jesus Christ is coming back to this earth again. They'll laugh at the whole idea. Why? The next phrase tells us. "Walking after their own lust." They don't want Christ to come. They don't want Christ to come and interfere with their way of living. They love their lust, they love their sins so much that they don't want Christ coming, and they cannot accept the idea that God is a God of judgment.

Now we know that God is a God of love. We know that God is a God of mercy, but the Bible also teaches that God is a God of wrath. He's a God of anger. Now that's not an emotional anger like you and I have. That's a divine anger at evil. A righteous indignation that Jesus had when He went into the Temple and drove out the money changers. The righteous indignation that He had when He turned on the Pharisees and called them all kinds of names in the 23rd chapter of Matthew. But primarily He accused them of being hypocrites. If there's anything God can't stand, it's a hypocrite. Scoffers, walking after their own lusts.

And then the Scripture says, "For this they willingly are ignorant of, that by the Word of God the heavens were of old, and the earth standing out of the water and in the water: whereby the world that then was, being overflowed with water, perished: but the heavens and the earth, which are now [right now] by the same word are kept in store, reserved unto fire against the day of judgment and perdition of ungodly men. But, beloved, be not ignorant of this one thing, that one day is with the Lord as a thousand years, and a thousand years as one day. The Lord is not slack concerning His promise, as some men count slackness, but is long suffering to us, not willing that any should perish, but that all should come to repentance.

"But remember this, the day of the Lord is going to come like a thief in the night, in which the heavens will pass away with a great noise, and the elements will melt with fervent heat, and the earth also, and the works that are therein shall be burned up."

Now in this passage of Scripture the Apostle Peter, under the inspiration of the Holy Spirit, is underlining something that is taught from Genesis to Revela-

THE DAY TO COME 121

tion—that a day of judgment is going to come. That the world is going to have to stand someday before the judgment of God. You will stand there as an individual, America will stand there as a nation, we'll stand there as a society, to give an account of our stewardship here.

Now we're having a debate in this country at the moment about our defense posture, the ABM, the MERV system. We've heard expressions from some of our scientists and some of those testifying in Washington about racial genocide, racial suicide. The word "Armageddon" is beginning to be used. The expression, "end of the human race"; the expression, "end of the world." Many of our scientists are pessimistic as to whether the world can stand very much longer. One scientist was quoted in the paper the other day as saying, "It's now possible to destroy the human race in a single day." But a Canadian scientist replied to him and said, "You're mistaken. It's now possible to destroy all of mankind in a single minute." Man himself could bring judgment upon the race by making a mistake.

Many historians are now emphasizing we're at the end. And so we find a great deal of pessimism and I think a part of the student rebellion, a part of the almost frantic quest for pleasure and having a good time, is the shadow of the possibility of the destruction of the human race. A lot of people have an idea, "Well, it's going to end. We might as well live it up and get what we can out of it."

And there are other students who say, "Well, maybe we can change it. Maybe we can do something," so they go out and start saying, "We're going to change the world." And they run right up against the same old problem that every generation has to face, and that's human nature. Lust, greed, hate and jealousy and all of those things which create the conditions for war.

And so the human race stands at this moment on the brink, on the threshold. Many of our leaders don't know the answer.

Now there are three elements even in modern theology. There is pessimism. Harry Emerson Fosdick was a pastor in this city for many years. In his sunset years he said this: "If one's thinking is dominated by the gigantic events of our generation, we cannot avoid despair." So we have a theology of despair. We have a theology of activism and we have a theology of hope. I belong to that group that has a theology of hope because my hope is not centered in this world or in what man is going to do or not going to do. My hope is centered in the person of our Lord Jesus Christ who, the Bible says, is going to come back some day and straighten the whole mess out. That's our hope: Jesus Christ.

I heard the story some time ago about a policeman right here in New York, and he saw a fellow standing on a bridge getting ready to jump in and end it all. The policeman went up to him and tried to talk him out of it and the fellow said, "No, my problems are so great and the problems of the world are so great that I'm just going to commit suicide." The policeman said, "All right, I'll make a deal with you. I'll give you five minutes to tell me why life is not worth living if you will give me five minutes to tell you why it is worth living." So they talked for ten minutes, and then they both jumped in.

And you know that's the way a lot of people are right here in New York. We rode with a taxi man yesterday here in this city, and he said, "Have you been down to hear that Graham fellow?" And I said, "Yes, I was down there the other night." And he said, "Where you from?" There were three of us in the taxi and I seemed to have gotten engaged in the conversation with him, but he couldn't see me. I was sitting on the left. I said, "North Carolina." He said, "Y'all got any problems down there?" I said, "We have a few." Well he said, "I want to tell you this city's in one lousy mess."

And then he began to tell us how bad it was.

But that's the feeling of a lot of people. They have the feeling that our problems can't be solved. There's no answer, no way out. Let's just give up.

I read the other day that we now have what is called a "suicide mentality." Well, you know, the Bible teaches that we're in for trouble, we're in for judgment. Convulsions, tribulations. But the Bible tells us that beyond that is the coming again of Christ when Christ is going to sit on the throne and rule the world. I'm looking forward to that day. I've been planning on it for years. And the Bible says that when we receive Christ as our Savior, we become members of His body, we become joint heirs with Christ, we become children of God, and we're going to reign with Him when He comes into His kingdom. Maybe Roger Hull will be Mayor of New York at that time. I don't know.

But you know Jesus Christ said something once. He said, as it was in the days of Noah, so shall it be in the day of the coming of the son of man. As it was before the flood, it's going to be again. As it was, so it will be. When conditions before the flood are repeated in history again, the end is near, said Jesus. As it was, it shall be.

Now, what happened in Noah's day? Take the fourth chapter, the fifth chapter, the sixth chapter of Genesis, and read it! First of all, travel was increasing very rapidly at that time. And the Bible says in Daniel 12:4 that one of the signs of the end of the age will be the increase of travel. Within my lifetime travel has moved from the automobile to the airplane, from the jet to the rockets. The Scripture says knowledge would increase, and that happened in Noah's day. Knowledge shall be increased. Knowledge is now doubling every ten years. Seventy-five percent of all the scientists who ever lived live now. In every field—so that now we have computers that can do 55 million transactions in one second. That's how knowledge is increasing.

It was also an age of technology. It says in the fourth chapter of Genesis, "And Zilah, she also bare Tubalcain, an instructor of every maker in brass and iron." You see, the discovery of brass and iron changed the world of Noah's day. It was a technological revolution. Look what technology is doing to our age. Look at the laser beam alone. One little ray of light can be used in all kinds of fields today, and it's going to revolutionize the world.

It was an age of entertainment. Musical instruments, the Bible says, were developed. Now that's why the Beatles stay on top. Did you know that? They've stayed on top a long time because they have a fantastic staff of experts making new instruments, new sounds and writing new music. Well, this was one of the things that happened in Noah's day. That's what it says: There were new musical instruments.

And also there was an abnormal emphasis on sex. Jesus said they were marrying and giving in marriage. They had become vile, decadent, and degenerate sexually. I can take you on a walk just a few blocks from here and show you pornographic pictures that will shock you.

As it was, so shall it be. Jesus said it happened once in history and a flood came. It will happen again in history and judgment will come, the last judgment.

And then there was the building of great cities. Genesis 4: "And Cain built a city and called the name of the city after the name of his son." That's the first mention of a city in the Bible. Now when God created man, He didn't put him in the middle of a city; He put him in a garden, and there are dangers to your spirit in city life that you don't find in the country. Morally and spiritually, there are temptations in the city that you don't face out in the small village and you don't face in rural areas. Seventy-five years ago 85 percent of our population lived in the rural areas. Today 75 percent of our population live in the urban areas. And so there's been a big change in America in the past few years. That was one of the signs; people moving to the cities in Noah's day, building great cities.

It was also a period of gluttony. Jesus said they were eating and drinking. They were interested in material things. They had very little appetite for God or for spiritual things. Their appetite was to fill their stomachs, satisfy their sex desires, when their curiosity at learning had become gluttony. Ever learning but never able to come to the truth, the Bible says. And, you see, we in America, we're continually dieting. We've got all kinds of pills and all kinds of diets to kill the appetite. We have a tremendous business in this country just to teach us how to quit eating and half of the world is trying to learn how to get started eating and, we in America and in Europe, in the affluent nations of the world, have become gigantic gluttons. Our dogs are better fed than millions of people in other parts of the world. That was one of the signs. That happened in Noah's day.

And then there was a world-wide violence. Pope Paul said a few days ago, "Violence, tensions, terrorism, reprisals, are sending a painful quiver throughout all of mankind." And he's right. Jesus said as it was in the days of Noah. You see, it says they were given to violence, they were given to lawlessness. Lawlessness had become world wide. People were revolting against all authority in those days. They're doing it today. It's not just an American problem. Somebody told me the other day that we're the most violent people in the world. Well, I'm not so sure about that. You go to Europe and things look fairly peaceful in certain places, but, remember, just in the last fifty years, they've had two wars that were extremely violent.

The whole world's violent. Go to China. My wife was born and reared in China, and her father had a great hospital in China for twenty-five years, and he said there was not a single day in twenty-five years that he didn't have people in his hospital whom he was treating for gunshot wounds. The highest he ever had was six hundred at one time—that he was treating for gunshot wounds. That sounds violent to me.

We're not the only violent people in the world. We're becoming violent, but wherever you find man living today, there's a violence in his heart, and it's a world-wide rebellion against authority and a world-wide lawlessness. Jesus said, "As it was, so shall it be." Another sign that the end is near.

Then there was a falling away of true faith. In Jude 11 it talks about those who have gone the way of Cain. Cain was one of the people who lived before Noah. He led the violence and the lawlessness that led to the flood in Noah's day. Now Cain believed in God as much as Abel, his brother, did. He was a believer in God. He wasn't an atheist; he was religious. The people of Noah's day were religious, but they had a wrong concept of religion. Cain believed that he could ignore God's plan of salvation and substitute a religion of good works, ethics, culture, and human righteousness, and it turned out to be nothing but humanism, and we've got a so-called sort of Christian humanism today that leaves out the Gospel. It leaves out the fact that man needs to have a personal relationship with Jesus Christ. And so today we have the same thing happening all over again. We're going the way of Cain, the way of humanism. In New Zealand the humanist society picketed our Crusade, carrying signs saying, "Don't let Billy Graham scare you." We need to fear God, not me.

The Bible teaches that toward the end of the age, it will be a time of peril, war, destruction, lawlessness, immorality so great that God will have to intervene and stop the whole thing lest we have racial genocide. Now listen to what Jesus said. Listen to what the Scripture says (Jesus said this in the 24th of Matthew): "For there shall be great tribulation such as was not since the beginning of the world to this time, nor will ever be again. And except those days should be shortened there should be no flesh saved, but for the sake of the elect, those days will be shortened." God said, "I'm not going to let the human race blow up in an atomic war. I'm going to stop it and I'm going to save it for the elect's sake."

That's why it's so important for believers, even though we're a small minority, to realize that for our sake the human race will be saved. For the sake of that small remnant and minority that believe, the human race will be rescued. That's what the Scripture says. Now you don't have to believe that. I'm just quoting Jesus. That's what Jesus said.

Those are passages you don't hear much preaching about. You know the preachers of judgment and Armageddon today are the scientists. Our scientists are the prophets. We in the pulpit are silent on the subject while the Bible is filled with it. We ought to be teaching the people and preaching to the people, warning the people, and showing the people the way to salvation.

Now in the midst of the generation of that day there

lived a man who believed in God, who walked with God. God said, "The thing has become so bad, and so decadent, and so violent, I'm going to destroy the human race and I'm going to start over again." Because, you see, when God created man, He gave him a gift He didn't give to His other creatures. He created man in His image and gave him freedom of choice. Man took this freedom, and it became license. He went his own way, rebelled against God, began to live his own life, and God said, "If you rebel against me you're going to die." Man has been suffering and dying ever since. "It's appointed unto man once to die and after that the judgment." Sin is rebellion against God. We're all rebels. The Bible says, "All have sinned and come short of the glory of God." We're all under the sentence of death. We're all under God's sentence. The wages of sin is death.

But in the midst of the generation of that day there lived a man, one man, who believed in God. His name was Noah. We've got people today who believe in God. There are people all over this world, in every country and in every city of the world, from Moscow to Peking, who believe in God. They may have to do it secretly, but they believe. When Mrs. Alliluyeva came to this country, the daughter of Joseph Stalin, she had been reared in intellectual atheism. She said, "I could no longer live in a world in which there was no God." She said, "All through the Soviet Union there are believers." She said even in the Communist Party there are believers. You see there are people who may declare their atheism for political reasons, but down inside have a secret faith and a secret belief that God is.

Noah believed in God in the midst of that crooked and perverse generation, and he dared to stand alone. He dared to stand up for something when everyone else was falling for anything. And I want to tell you, to stand up at one of our modern universities today and say "I believe in God" and lift up a Bible and say, "I believe this book to be the inspired word of God," takes a lot of courage. And there's many a Christian professor who leads a lonely life on campus. And there's many a student in a class who leads a lonely life because he believes in Christ and he believes in God, and he believes in the Bible. But they're there. God has His people scattered all over the world and a Crusade like this brings a lot of them together. And many of you are going to go back and you're going to have to fight a lot of battles with yourself and with others.

He dared to stand alone. And that's what Jesus meant when He said, "Take up the Cross and follow me. Bear my reproach. Be willing to go outside the camp with me and live where it's unpopular." Are you willing to do that? He said, count the cost. You may have to stand alone. Noah stood alone and God came to him one day and said, "Noah, I'm going to destroy the human race with a flood. I'm going to cause it to rain forty days and forty nights. I want you to build a ship and save your household and save the animals," and the Bible says that Noah believed God. Noah didn't argue with God and say, "Well, Lord, there's no scientific evidence that any flood's coming. I haven't heard 'Walter Cronkite' mention it on the news yet. I haven't heard any scientist say anything about it at 'Columbia or Stanford.'" The Bible says by faith Noah, being warned of God of things not seen as yet [no evidence seen as yet], moved with fear [notice what moved him, fear], prepared the ark.

Now if ever a generation had a right to be moved by fear and get right with God, it's our generation. The headlines are screaming it to us. They're preaching to us every day. I think it was Chief Justice Warren who said he always turns to the sports section first to read what man is accomplishing, and then he turns to the front page to see man's failures. And there's a lot of truth in that.

God said, "Noah, I want you to build this ship 450 feet long and 45 feet wide, and 75 feet high, three stories, one window, one side door, and I want you to get it ready as quick as you can." Noah began to build. The people laughed and sneered and thought he'd gone mad, but, of course, he paid top wages and they worked for him and helped him. But they laughed at him. And during all that period of time that they were building this ship [it took 120 years to build it], Noah was preaching, warning the people, "repent, judgment is coming, believe." But they laughed and sneered and did not believe.

Now during that period of time, God could have sent the judgment earlier but He didn't do it. God had a secret that you can go back home and figure out. The oldest man who ever lived was 969 years. Now why was Methuselah the oldest man who ever lived? Have you ever thought about that? His name means—"When he is dead it shall be sent." As long as Methuselah lived, God would not send that flood. The day that Methuselah died, the flood came. God used him as a symbol of His love, His grace, His mercy and His long suffering, hoping that mankind would repent of their sins and turn to Him before it was too late. Methuselah just kept on living. God's patience, God's love, and Methuselah stand forever in the Bible as illustrations of the love, and the mercy, and the grace of God. God could have judged them years earlier, but He didn't do it.

Now Methuselah kept on living and the day he died, the flood came. "When he is dead, it shall be sent."

Now, what is God using in our generation. All right, you can read it. 2 Thessalonians 2:6-7. The Holy Spirit is God's restraining power in our world, and as long as the Holy Spirit is here in mighty power, working as we've seen Him in this Garden, God is going to be long-suffering and merciful, not willing, not desiring that any should be lost but that all should be saved.

We are living in a period of God's mercy. We are breathing, and we are living by the mercy and the grace of God. The Holy Spirit is God's mighty restraining power. But I know some theologians who are saying that the Holy Spirit in His restraining grace throughout the world may be in the process of being removed. The Holy Spirit's activity in bringing individuals to Christ is accelerating because people are being converted all over the world to Christ. The Bible says as we move toward the end of history that Gospel preaching will increase and the Gospel will be heard all around the world. Today, for the first time, it's being heard around the world by radio and television and by the printed page. When Frank Borman read the Word of God in outer space, it was heard by millions around the world. The Holy Spirit is God's restraining power. At the moment the Holy Spirit is removed, this earth is going to turn into almost hell. And the Bible says that Christ is going to come back.

You want to read about when He comes? I'll read it to you. There are so many passages in the Bible that deal with the coming again of Christ that it's almost impossible to read them all. But turn to the 19th chapter of Revelation. Listen to this. Beginning at verse 11. "And I saw heaven opened; and behold a white horse; and he that sat upon him was called Faithful and True, and in righteousness he doth judge and make war. His eyes were as a flame of fire, and on his head were many crowns; and he had a name written that no man knew but he himself. And he was clothed with a vesture dipped in blood: and his name is called The Word of God. And the armies which were in heaven followed him upon white horses, clothed in fine linen, white and clean. And out of his mouth goeth a sharp sword, that with it he should smite the nations: and he shall rule them with a rod of iron: and he treadeth the winepress of the fierceness and wrath of Almighty God. And he hath on his vesture and on his thigh a name written, King of Kings, and Lord of Lords."

Yes, He's coming back. Next time not as the little baby at Bethlehem, but as the mighty King of Kings and Lord of Lords. And He Himself said He's coming back to intervene in history to save the world from destroying itself because God loves the world. And He's going to come in judgment, and He's going to rule. He'll be the ruler.

The future ruler of the world is not capitalism or Communism. It's Christ. He's the one who's going to rule. He's Kings of Kings and Lord of Lords.

Jesus said He will come as a thief in the night because, you see, just before the Scripture that I read there, you can turn to 1 Thessalonians 4 and there we read that He's going to come for the believers. All the believers are going to be resurrected. Yes, I'm going to see my father some day. I'm going to see my loved ones some day. I'm going to be reunited with them some day. We're going to see them again. And the Scripture says, "Two shall be in the field, one taken and one left behind. Two women will be grinding at the mill. One taken and one left behind." He said, "You must always be ready for you do not know what time the Son of man is coming back."

No, we don't know the time but we read the signs of the times, and the signs of the times would indicate that we're approaching that glorious moment when Christ is going to come back again. And you know what the Scripture says about it? It says "Comfort one another with these words." Now we don't have much comfort today. The fact that Christ is coming back should be of great comfort to every believer in the world. We've got a hope. We've got a program. We've got a future. The future belongs to us. We're on the winning side. Let's comfort each other with those words.

And then the Scripture says something else. It says this hope purifies you. In other words, this is a part of our sanctification. Growing in the grace and knowledge of Christ. Our hope centered in His appearing should cause us to live pure lives, obedient lives.

And then the Scripture says that we should watch. That's what we're doing tonight. We're watching. And, you know, I've gotten in the habit of going to bed at night and thinking just before I go to bed, "What if He should come tonight!" I wake up in the morning and, the first thought I have is, "I wonder if He's going to come today." Oh, I'd like to see Him come. What a day that's going to be! All of our aches and pains are going to be behind us. All of our tears are going to be behind us. All of our problems are going to be solved. What a day that's going to be! And Jesus is going to rule and the problems, the social problems that we are wrestling with and battling with now—trying to patch them up and solve them as best we can—they're all going to be totally solved. The race problem will be solved. The poverty problem will be solved. The war problem will be solved. There'll be no more war. What a day that's going to be when we stand with Him in eternity!

And then Jesus said, "Be ready." Are you prepared for

that day? Does Christ live in your heart? Are you prepared for the day of judgment? Should Christ come tonight, are you prepared? The Scripture says, "Prepare to meet thy God." How do you prepare? You prepare first of all by being certain that you know Christ is your Savior, by repenting of your sins.

Now what does repentance mean? It means that you're willing to say, "God, I've sinned. I'm willing to give up my sin. I'm willing to change my way of living." That's repentance.

And secondly, by faith you receive Christ as your Savior. You're not trusting in your good works; you're not trusting in anything except Jesus Christ and what He did at the Cross for your salvation. Nothing else.

And you must receive Him by faith and believe. And then you must be willing to follow Him and serve Him. It means that you start living a disciplined life under the Lordship of Christ. It means that you serve Him in every little thing, every day. You see, God's keeping books on you. He's got a computer system all His own, and He sees the little things nobody ever praises you for. How many of you do things that are really good things, and nobody ever sees them, and nobody ever praises you, and you'd like to have a little praise? He's keeping a record. It's all there. Serve Him in a thousand ways every day.

I'm going to ask you to receive Christ right now. I'm going to ask hundreds of you to get up out of your seat right now and say by coming down here, "I do receive Christ. I accept Him as my Lord and my Savior. I want my sins forgiven. I want to know I'm going to heaven."

As you can see, hundreds of people are coming from every part of this Garden to make their commitment to Christ. You can make that same commitment in your home or in a bar, a hotel lobby, or wherever you may be watching. You can say an eternal "yes" to Christ, and He will forgive your sin and change your life.

Delivered June 22, 1969